SOVIET UNION
1991

0 100 200   400   600   800   1000
KILOMETERS

0 100 200   400   600   800   1000
STATUTE MILES

TWO-POINT EQUIDISTANT PROJECTION

BROKEN EMPIRE

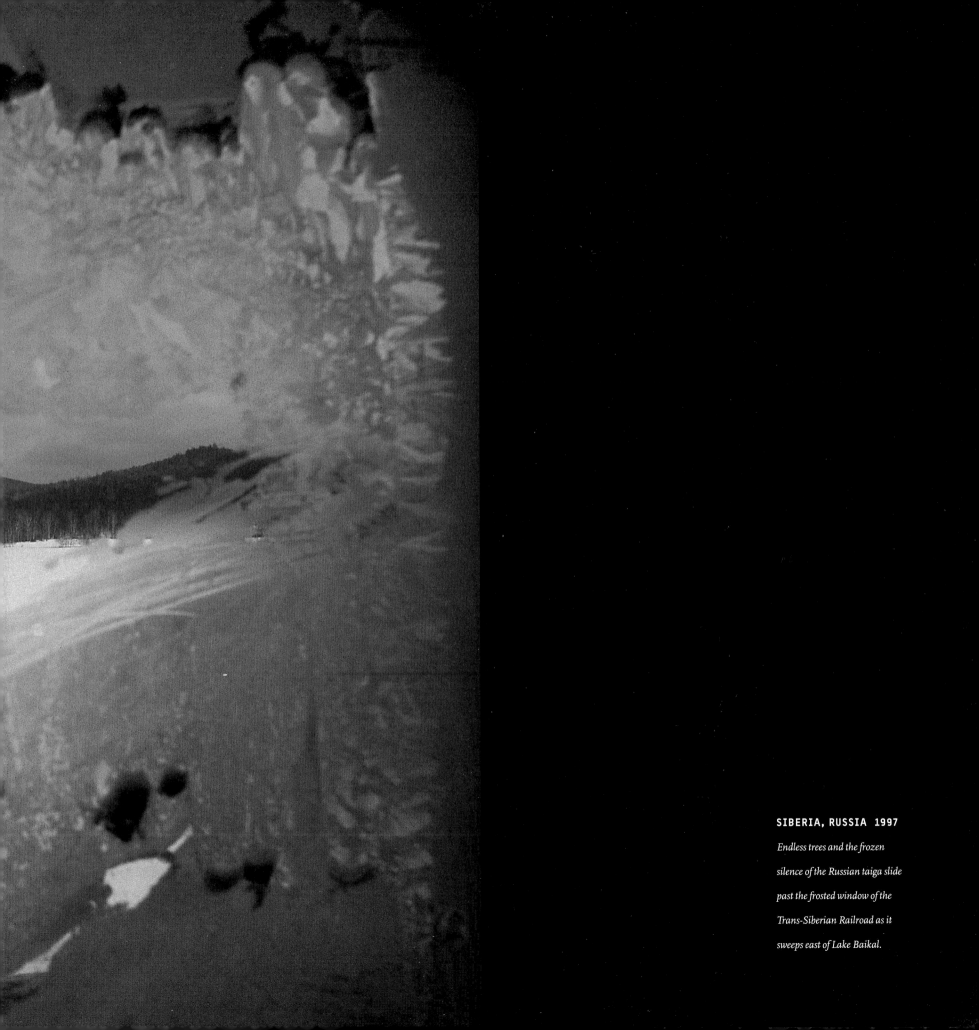

SIBERIA, RUSSIA 1997

Endless trees and the frozen silence of the Russian taiga slide past the frosted window of the Trans-Siberian Railroad as it sweeps east of Lake Baikal.

Benetton megastore: A 21,000-square-foot merchandizing behemoth, filled with Italian flair, replaced the state-run Natasha department store.

MOSCOW 1992

A smoking sentry stands guard in Krasnoprenenskaya Square as his partners sell shots of homemade wine to thirsty Muscovites. With the end of the Soviet era, these moonshiners and others from the Caucasus —four days away by car—were free to bring their business to the Russian capital.

KIEV, UKRAINE 1992

Devout Russian Orthodox queue up to collect holy water from a spring about to be blessed by the metropolitan of their church. Such a religious gathering was hard to find during the communist regime.

MOSCOW 1996

Forced in former times to hide
their sexual preferences, gay
men can now meet openly at
clubs like Moscow's Chance.

VLADIVOSTOK,

RUSSIA 1997

Russians flock to Vladivostok

in summer months to vacation

beside the Sea of Japan.

BROKEN EMPIRE

GERD LUDWIG

TEXT BY
FEN MONTAIGNE

NATIONAL GEOGRAPHIC INSIGHT

WASHINGTON, D.C.

CONTENTS

FOREWORD BY TATYANA TOLSTAYA

At a store in Moscow, two boys around ten years old were eyeing a counter full of delicacies.

"You know," one said, "my mom told me there used to be lines to buy food."

"Lines?" the other replied.

The boys laughed over this, incredulous. They had never seen lines, except maybe for movie tickets. It occurred to me these boys were probably born in 1991, at the height of the most frightening period of shortages that I can remember. Stores in both Moscow and St. Petersburg were literally empty, so empty, in fact, that retailers took to covering up the indecency of bare counters with dolls or plastic flowers arranged here and there along their shelves. Whatever meager goods did appear would be subject to distribution rules. Kasha, for instance, would be limited to two kilograms a customer. Oranges would be sold only to persons with passports attesting to their Moscow residence permits. In pre-reforms Russia, it wasn't only in the streets that people stood in lines. People hoping to buy a government apartment would wait in line for ten to fifteen years; buying a cooperative apartment also meant waiting for years on end. There were long lists of people waiting to buy shoes or rugs. Of course, there were privileges, too. My father-in-law, for instance, a decorated general, was notified that in two years he would be able to purchase an iron. Once I found a postcard in my mailbox notifying the former owner of my apartment, who had died two years earlier, that it was finally time for him to come pick up his *Feia* (Fairy) washing machine.

An eventful and grueling decade of reforms has inverted the old relationship of goods to money: Today, the stores are full—people's pockets are empty. Prices are European, but the official average monthly wage is $100 to $150 in Moscow, and much lower in the provinces. The official minimum monthly wage is $10, while the minimum living standard—also official—is about $35. Meanwhile, a third of the country lives below that minimum, or below the poverty line. Statistical averages, of course, do not reflect the true situation: In reality, people are in some ways worse off, in others, better. For starters, people don't report their shadow incomes, both honest (from tutoring, say, or peddling at marketplaces) and dishonest (bribes, pilfering). Our shadow economy, meanwhile, is enormous, like the underside of an iceberg. For another thing, in most families there is one person who earns enough to support all the other members. By an unspoken bargain between the government and the public, the authorities turn a blind eye to the shadow dimension of the economy, while the people regard corrupt bureaucrats as an unavoidable evil, and their grumbling about them remains for the most part just talk. The result is a certain equilibrium, one that is very hard to disturb without disrupting the system that currently helps people to survive. Those who are unable to adapt to that parallel economy and find a place in it for themselves (pensioners, disabled persons, refugees)—these people live in poverty and hardship. It must be said that we've seen regular attempts on the part of the government to rehabilitate our society, to make the economy transparent and rationalize our tax system. These attempts are resisted by both bureaucrats and the public, which habitually mistrusts the authorities.

The role of the press (the media) in this process is an interesting one. On the one hand, people regard the press as itself corrupt, and therefore not to be believed. On the other hand, the exposés published in the press only reinforce people's conviction that everyone around them is corrupt and there's no conceivable solution—and therefore it's pointless to change anything about their own lifestyles.

Assessing the situation in Russia is difficult: It all depends on how you define your living standards and expectations. From the 1920s to the early 1960s life in Russia was unquestionably many times more horrible than it is today. But those who rail against the troubles they have now were young in those years. And so it seems to them that life was better back then: The myth of a golden age, after all, is eternal. As for the relative prosperity of the 1960s and '70s—something else that all of us recall—it was unsustainable, and by the time Gorbachev launched *perestroika* it had already ended. Yet to the people who are struggling to get by today, it seems that this illusory abundance was ruined by Gorbachev himself.

Poverty and the lack of rights, as always, are being exploited by the communists. But their demagogic, hysterical speeches and calls forrevolution only serve to conceal their true intentions, which are to recover their former political power and the money that went with it. They have no economic program. What they offer up instead is chimerical nostrums and fantasies. "The answer is to print up bales of money and distribute it to the poor." "The market is bad for agriculture," and so on and so on. And the more impoverished and ignorant their audience is, the more eagerly it listens to these charlatans.

During the years they were in power, the Communists disrupted and destroyed everything they possibly could, and there was no freedom of speech. Today there is no more censorship in Russia, and heinous crimes against society and humanity are coming to light, crimes with origins in the remote Soviet past. Naturally, the Communists wash their hands of any responsibility for them and pin the blame on the new and, in many respects, imperfect regime. Unfortunately, their arguments are often echoed by the Western press, which has long since lost any interest in an accurate analysis of Russia's problems. Over the past five years I've had to read so many stunningly idiotic statements and outright lies about Russia in the pages of authoritative Western publications that I can fully understand why Russian society is disenchanted with Western thinking in general.

Often what seems disastrous turns out to be your deliverance. Under the Communists, Russian industry was senseless, economically untenable, absolutely uncompetitive, and very nearly ruinous to our country's environment. Under the new regime there was a sharp industrial decline, factories closed, and people lost their jobs. This occasioned a lot of gloomy speculation that Russia was done for. Few people noticed, however, that this development had done us some good. Over the years of involuntary industrial downtime, the environment improved substantially. Where the soil had been barren, grass and trees took root, the air grew cleaner, and in the fields flowers that our old people hadn't seen since childhood reappeared. Meanwhile, people who had been engaged in the pointless manufacture of absolutely unneeded products found work in other areas. Granted, people want to arrive at prosperity quickly. Granted, their impatience at times takes on misshapen, criminal forms. But the fact is that in Russia there is now a slowly but steadily growing middle class, and that is perhaps our chief reason to be optimistic. The future belongs to patient, competent, and diligent workers like these.

Russia is an astonishing country, capable of regeneration in the most unlikely and adverse circumstances. And when I'm saddened by what I see happening around me, I recall the dirt-poor, rightless existence I used to lead in pre-reforms Russia, and hear again the incredulous laughter of two boys, two future Russian citizens, for whom the Soviet past seems like a stupid fabrication, like a bizarre fairy tale. And it's good that it seems like that to them. ■

MOSCOW 1987

Awed by their imposing surroundings, two young girls whisper together in the foyer of the legendary Moscow Arts Theater.

INTRODUCTION

A remote German village in 1951. The room is dark and cold. But as a small child, tucked in bed between my parents' bodies, I am oblivious to the poverty of the cramped space that serves as our kitchen, bedroom, and living room. In the darkness, I listen to the sad, soothing voice of my father as he conjures images of endless winter landscapes; he and other soldiers battling their way through snowstorms; and people hiding from them in stables and barns.

Our small family moves, the surroundings change, but the stories continue. "Vati, in your stories the people are never bad. Why did you fight them?" I ask. "It was war, my son...." It was not until I grew older that I began to grasp the darkness behind the stories—that the landscapes were stained with blood, the soldiers dying, and the people hiding Russians filled with fear. And that my father did not tell these just as bedtime stories but to shed himself of terrible memories, like a snake shedding a skin. But the memories, like a snakeskin, always grew back, and he had to tell his stories once again.

For generations both of my parents' families, ethnic Germans, had lived in a part of Bohemia known as the Sudetenland, where nationalities could change overnight as borders were arbitrarily redrawn by shifting powers. Born a citizen of Austria-Hungary, my father was designated a Czechoslovakian citizen after World War I and later drafted into the Czech Army. When Europe's leaders conceded to Hitler's demands to annex Czechoslovakia in 1939, my father went from being a Czech soldier one day to a German soldier the next. As part of the Sixth German Army that invaded the Soviet Union in 1942, he battled through the Ukraine into southern Russia. In the desperate winter of 1942-43 at Stalingrad, the tables finally turned, and the Russians began to decimate the German forces. My father was lucky; he was among the last soldiers evacuated.

But as a young teenager in the mid-1960s, I didn't see it that way. A member of the first postwar generation of Germans, I was painfully aware of the political crimes of my parents' generation and of the suffering Germany had inflicted on the world. Full of guilt, I compensated for my feelings by glorifying everything that Germany had wished to destroy. Particularly Russia. Unable to separate people from political systems, I dismissed all evidence of the Soviet Union's repressive government as Western propaganda.

Later, in my 30s, during the height of the Cold War, I found myself on assignment for European magazines in the Soviet Union. I was still so stricken with guilt about Germany's role in the war that I willingly adhered to the unspoken Soviet mandate to photograph only positive aspects of life under communism. While my images were genuine attempts to mirror the Russian soul, they ignored economic realities.

Finally, in the late 1980s, Gorbachev's *glasnost*—his call for openness in every part of life—lifted the veil and confronted me with the social and political realities of a country that had been under totalitarian rule for seven decades. At last, I was able to separate the political system from the people and capture a different, more complete vision from the one I had been focused on for so long.

IN 1991, ONLY TWO WEEKS AFTER the August coup that unseated Gorbachev, I was in the U.S.S.R. on assignment for NATIONAL GEOGRAPHIC. During Gorbachev's tenure, the disastrous condition of the Russian economy was slowly becoming known to the rest of the world, but its most extreme manifestations were still shielded from the Western media. When I began to portray the new Russia in the early '90s I had two avenues to explore: the transformation of a society from a state-controlled to a market economy at manic speed; and the social and economic conditions that had prevailed for generations, hidden from outside eyes.

Gradually, I discovered that, though Soviet rulers had professed concern for workers and respect for nature, they destroyed both with their environmental recklessness. The bald children of Chornobyl and the limbless children of Moscow were part of a deeply disturbing truth: Birth defects and infant death—not just in the vicinity of the atomic catastrophe but even in the empire's once proud capital—strike the peoples of this land at twice the rate found in industrial nations of the West.

While researching a story on pollution in the former Soviet Union, I came across reports of children and pregnant women being diagnosed with a strange breakdown of the immune system in the industrial city of Sumqayit in Azerbaijan. Flying into Baku in the summer of 1993, I found that city in turmoil as rebel troops approached. Drunken soldiers with machine guns occupied several rooms on our floor in the hotel. When we drove to Sumqayit, we were overcome by a stinging, noxious odor as we approached the city. Our eyes began to water uncontrollably, and we tasted the sulfur fumes expelled from chemical plants in the area. Along the way we were stopped by militia several times, even briefly detained. Yet we still managed to bypass local bureaucrats and gain access to the children's hospital, because its director felt an obligation to show the world what was happening to the children of his country.

One of them, a five-month-old infant boy named Nurlan Musayev, showed severe symptoms of toxic dystrophy, anemia, gastrointestinal infection, and a total breakdown of the immune system. Locals called his condition, endemic to the region, "chemical AIDS." His parents, both 22, were refugees from the Nagorno-Karabakh conflict and lived in a shack close to the chemical plant, where they worked. I began to photograph Nurlan, lying motionless as a group of doctors struggled to find a vein in his twiglike arm to start an IV. The sight was heartbreaking.

As a photographer, it is my responsibility to witness events playing out before my camera. Normally, in extreme situations like this one, I am able to both empathize and endure the pain, because, by holding my camera and making an image, I have a creative outlet, a means of channeling whatever horror I am experiencing into the picture. But on this day I had to leave the scene. Once in the doctor's room, I revived enough to begin to wonder whether I had got the shot. I asked one of the doctors to escort me back to the emergency room. He brusquely informed me that the "body was already in the morgue." I thought of my own young son in Los Angeles, and, once outside, I broke down in tears.

Pollution, poor health care and poor nutrition, alcohol and drug abuse are all taking their toll in the former superpower. When health care in the Soviet Union was at its best during the mid-sixties, life expectancy had briefly exceeded that of the United States. But the situation has deteriorated precipitously. Today the life expectancy of a Russian male is 58 years, a figure below the average for Latin America, Asia, the Middle East, and East Africa.

In 1992, at Hospital 21 in Volgograd, I witnessed the human impact of bad health care—and I experienced one of the most shocking and poignant moments of my career. Three years earlier, a sailor who had contracted AIDS in Africa returned to Russia and was treated in this hospital. The needles and syringes were re-used, and as a result 288 children, ranging in age from one month to 14 years old, had been infected. By the time I arrived, several children had already died. I attended a Christmas party organized by the Salvation Army for about 50 of the doomed children and their families. For some of the victims, this would be their last Christmas. The adults sat with tears in their eyes as the children played and laughed and opened their gifts, innocent of their fate.

PHOTOGRAPHING IN A COUNTRY that for decades had practiced censorship with its own media, I was confronted with a range of problems that shifted as the years and assignments passed. For a foreign photographer during the Brezhnev era, even permits to shoot candle-lit Orthodox churches and goose-stepping soldiers in front of the Kremlin had been difficult to obtain. But once I found the appropriate contact in the Soviet bureaucratic pyramid, one benevolent nod from above was enough to trigger a chain of permissions. With the collapse of the system came a brief window of opportunity for nearly unrestricted access. When I arrived back in the dissolving empire in 1992, however, I found myself lost in a maze of intricate relationships: Liberal-minded bosses in the 15 capitals of the newly independent republics were willing to oblige me, but bureaucrats at the local levels remained reluctant.

Today, access is often more restricted than at the height of the Cold War. Two layers of bureaucracy exist on top of each other. The state bureaucracy requires official permits to enter various regions and areas, while the newly established capitalist bureaucracy restricts access to anything privately owned. These intertwined systems form a Gordian knot that can often be cut only by a stiff bribe.

MOSCOW 1987

Renowned actress Anastasia
Vertinskaya ranked among the
few Russians privileged enough
to own a car in the late 1980s.
Her father, also a famous actor
and director, received a death
sentence at one time from
Stalin but was later pardoned.

My assistants and I once spent hours at a designated ministry trying to obtain a permit to photograph in a prison. The official in charge insisted over a period of several hours that the request would be denied. Then he offered a solution: For $1,500 a day we could enjoy the exclusive treatment of being locked up and treated like prisoners. And I could have my camera equipment to photograph. We politely declined. Later that day we got a call from a mysterious stranger who offered us access to the required prison for a bottle of cognac. Done deal. *Na zdorovye!*

Even after obtaining every conceivable permit for an assignment, I have been detained and interrogated. My suspicious acts included photographing a bridge in Novosibirsk while shooting a Trans-Siberian Railroad story; wearing a ghost costume on Halloween in Kiev; climbing a scaffolding on a Sunday morning in Moscow; and taking pictures of the harbor in Vladivostok. Although annoying and extremely time consuming, none of these incidents ever escalated into personal danger. Except for the aftermath to the arrest in Vladivostok. A year later, as I was shooting the Trans-Siberian Railroad, I ran into my former jailor, Yevgeny, on the train. He recognized me, and, consumed with guilt over his role in my arrest, he insisted on making it up to me by sharing his bottle of moonshine. I lived through it. *Na zdorovye!*

LIFE-THREATENING MOONSHINE, freezing temperatures, hotel rooms with no heat or far too much, restaurant managers who steal my birthday dinner, mafia cab drivers, cold green chicken dinners, communist guards who break my assistant's nose....Why do I return? For *dusha* and dusha only.

Dusha is that enigmatic Russian inner world, expansive and authentic, full of a compassion and great deep suffering that tempers and purifies. It is an unconscious drive...a belief in the inexplicable and the mysterious. It is people reading books in forests. All-night conversations. Drunks pondering the meaning of life. It's not the Western search for well-being, it does not acknowledge harsh reality, it is the antithesis of everyday modern life. It is forgiveness, empathy, conscience, and the ability of humans to partake in the Divine. It is the Russian soul.

Once, I was asked by my driver, a man named Volodya, if we could stop and see his mother who lived nearby in a remote village along the Don River—an area few foreigners ever visit. Volodya's mother, warm and hospitable as most Russians are, insisted I join in the feast she prepared for her son. Her house was small, the kitchen, bedroom, and living room all one space decorated with old tapestries and carpets. We crowded around the table, which was pushed close to the bed where the mother sat. A full blue moon shone through the one small window as we ate and drank for hours, exchanging life stories. Babushka was laughing, spirited, glowing, loving life.

She had mentioned her husband several times, and yet there was no sign of him. When I asked where he was, her face changed briefly as if searching for an answer. She said, "He left one day and never came back." Something made me inquire further. "When was that?" She quietly answered, "In 1942...the war." The conversation continued as if nothing had happened, but I was disturbed by her answer. It took me some courage, but I finally asked her how she felt about having me, a German, in her home. As Russians often do, she answered with a story.

"In 1942 I was at home alone with my children when there was a knock on the door. When I opened it, a tall blond German officer with blue eyes stood in front of me. Volodya and his sister were trying to hide behind my apron. The officer demanded *'Milch'* and *'Butter.'* I pointed at the children, trying to explain to him that I needed my milk and butter for the *'kinder.'* He looked at my daughter and asked her name. I told him it was Maria. He stood there for a second...as if he were looking through Maria. Then, without a word, he turned and walked away. But before he turned, I thought I saw his eyes fill with tears." *Russkaya Dusha.* ∎

ONE THE WAY IT WAS

My first impression of Moscow, shared by many who visited the capital in its communist days, was that I had landed in a metropolis under blackout. Though not yet four in the afternoon, it was already dark as I drove into the city from Sheremetyevo Airport. Moscow's wide avenues, flanked by imposing Stalinist apartment blocks, were a universe of grays and browns. Through the murk, figures in bulky coats and fur *shapkas* scurried in and out of shops whose windows cast a feeble glow. Above this dismal vista, on Gorky Street, I saw illuminated red stars suspended in the sky above the Kremlin towers—communist baubles startling in their brilliance. It was November 1989, before the Berlin Wall fell, and a feeling took hold of me then that has not diminished in the ensuing years, a sense that I had entered a great, damaged, alien—and compelling—domain. As Moscow correspondent for the *Philadelphia Inquirer,* I would call this home for the next several years.

In the morning, my sense of having landed on another planet was heightened as I walked out of my temporary apartment onto October Square, where a statue of the man himself, Comrade Lenin, strode into the shining future, coattails flying in his wake. The streets looked much as they had for decades. A few cars passed, the black Volga sedans of the Communist Party apparatchiks emitting hollow growls as chauffeurs shifted gears. Signs of commerce were scarce. Newspapers and ice cream were on sale at kiosks for a few kopecks apiece. Occupying the first floor of the stone-and-concrete apartment buildings, stores were offering little more than spaghetti, jars of Bulgarian tomatoes, milk, blocks of frozen fish, and rolls of bologna. Today, I'm grateful I had the opportunity to see Moscow's old exterior, for its spareness and order eloquently communicated both the security, and the yearnings, that the U.S.S.R. created in its citizens.

A few days later I witnessed the expression of those yearnings in a scene that now seems impossibly quaint, particularly given the reckless brush with capitalism Russia has experienced in the ensuing years. Near Gorky Park, as a wet snow fell on muddy sidewalks and the late afternoon gloom descended on the capital, I spied a vision: It was a bright, gold-and-green trailer. Inside, bathed in yellow light, young workers dressed in colorful uniforms moved briskly about. On the front was a sign that read: "Nathan's Famous Frankfurters. Since 1916."

This was the era when Western businesses were just beginning to trickle into the Russian capital. A New Jersey entrepreneur had come up with the inspiration to ship a Nathan's trailer to Moscow and sell American hot dogs, chili, and hot chocolate to Russians, who were then accustomed to standing in interminable lines for delicacies like bananas, oranges, or cheese.

As I approached the trailer, a swarm of people was savoring steaming chili and kosher frankfurters. "I have not experienced anything so tasty, so quick, and the people who served us were so polite," said Galina Smirnova, 25. "You do not see this often in Moscow. This is our first time at Nathan's, but it is not our last. It has given us enormous pleasure." Passersby stopped and stared at the trailer, as if it had fallen from heaven. "Where is this from?" one man inquired. "America," came the reply. "Ahhh."

Then he got in line.

OF COURSE, BRINGING HOT DOGS and hamburgers to the U.S.S.R. was the easy part. In late 1989, Mikhail Gorbachev's *perestroika* and *glasnost* had peaked. The apex of that euphoria had come early that year, when the freely elected Congress of People's Deputies held historic, televised sessions during which some members denounced the tyranny of the old communist regimes and called for quickening the march toward capitalism and democracy. Breathing life into the moribund Soviet system was always a daunting task for Gorbachev, but pursuing his policy of glasnost, or openness, proved to be far simpler than carrying out his perestroika, or restructuring. Reluctantly, the Communist Party's fossilized elders tolerated a discussion of the Soviet system's shortcomings, but implementing economic reforms or giving the country's 15 republics more autonomy was another matter indeed.

The Soviet Union was stuck in this rut—lots of talk, no action—when I arrived in late 1989, and the masses were weary, looking for signs of improvement in their daily lives.

During a foray to the southern fringes of the capital, where laundry flapped on the balconies of high-rise apartments that sprawled to the horizon, I talked with young housewives who despaired at the limbo. "As much as we talk, it seems we can't find a way out," said 26-year-old Annette Gadyeva. "People looked for material progress to confirm the words of Gorbachev, but they got none. Now they don't even have soap."

Another young mother, pushing her four-month-old baby in a stroller, added, "This process is wearing people out."

In eary February 1990, after a brief visit to the United States, I returned to Russia with my wife, who was three months pregnant, and our one-year-old daughter. A day after we arrived, the Communist Party voted to end its 70-year monopoly on power and allow a multiparty political system. From then on, for the next two years, I watched as the Soviet Union spun apart at an ever accelerating rate.

Although it wasn't always clear at the time, it's evident now that Gorbachev was trying to do the impossible—essentially, to get the U.S.S.R. half pregnant with reform. He wanted to give the country's 15 republics more autonomy but not outright independence. Yet once Moscow loosened the bonds on places like Lithuania and Armenia, they were determined to break away completely. Gorbachev pushed the Communist Party to reform itself and share power, but once most Russians sensed that the party of Lenin was giving ground, they wanted to scrap it altogether.

Years later, when the Soviet safety net was shredded and tens of millions of Russians lived below the poverty level, a wave of nostalgia for the good old days under communism swept a sizable segment of the population. But they had short memories. In the dying days of the Soviet Union, it was difficult to find anyone—other than party apparatchiks—who would defend the communist system. Throughout 1990 and 1991, I covered numerous rallies in Moscow where hundreds of thousands of people marched to protest the privilege and corruption of the Communist Party. In other cities, protests led to the resignations of old-style party bosses. After 70 years of oppressive party rule, after decades of watching party hacks treating themselves to the best food, apartments, and cars while most Soviets struggled to get by in a country more Third World than First, the common man was fed up.

"Thieves," 57-year-old Volgograd steelworker Vladimir Serov told me in the winter of 1990. He had supported protests that ousted the region's top party officials. "Everything for themselves, nothing for the workers. We should do away with these miserable people."

For those of us tracking the centrifugal forces pulling apart the U.S.S.R., Lithuania was like a second home. It seemed that every other week I was boarding an overnight train for the capital, Vilnius, where Lithuanians were bolting from the Soviet Union so fast it made everyone's head spin, including Gorbachev's. Those overnight train trips to some corner of the disintegrating Soviet Empire are a central memory of those years for me. The slick black ice on the platform of the Moscow train station; the acrid smell of the coal used to heat samovars; the sour odor of damp clothes, garlic, Bulgarian tobacco, and vodka that assaulted you as you entered the car; the sweet tea served by dour conductresses—these sensations seem every bit as vivid today as they were a decade ago. On one such trip, from Vilnius to Moscow, I was settling into my first-class compartment, relieved that no one would be joining me in its narrow confines, when the door opened and in walked a striking woman—tall, blond, blue-eyed, exquisite cheekbones. She took off her long, suede coat, stowed her bag, and sat down on the opposite bed as the train lurched out of the station. I had been in the country only a few months and struggled to speak with her in Russian. When the time came to sleep, she grabbed her coat, disappeared into the bathroom down the corridor, returned, took off her coat, and stood there in a low-cut nightgown as I tried, with mixed success, to avert my eyes. As she crawled into her berth, not two feet from mine, I was certain that she was a KGB plant and that a camera was running in the next compartment, recording our every move. I did not sleep well. The next morning, as the Russian beauty and I walked off the train, my pregnant wife was there, holding our first child in her arms. After saying good-bye to my fellow traveler, I tried to explain to my wife how I had innocently slept next to the stranger all night. To this day I can't decide whether her appearance was happenstance or a KGB attempt to probe for my particular weaknesses.

In February 1990, the roughly 3.5 million people of Lithuania elected a new parliament. Within weeks, it had declared the nation's independence. I was standing in the parliament's chambers in Vilnius, and when the legislators pulled a curtain over the huge hammer-and-sickle communist emblem in the hall and hoisted the red-, yellow-, and-green Lithuanian flag in its place, I experienced the first of what would be a string of "Holy shit!" moments during my three-year Moscow tour. Lithuania had become the first republic out the door, and it was clearly not going to be the last. My colleagues and I looked at each other: We had just seen the first pillar of the Soviet Empire crumble.

In Moscow, Gorbachev—caught between the forces of reform and reaction—acted like a leader "with his foot on the accelerator and the brake at the same time," in the words of one Soviet legislator. His prime minister, Nikolai Ryzhkov, announced that the government might lift decades-old price controls on such staples as bread and pasta. The public reaction was swift, as I saw the following day in Moscow's grocery stores. In a matter of hours, panicked shoppers stripped shelves of anything even remotely edible. The government backed down, and people breathed a sigh of relief that they could continue buying bread at prices that had not risen appreciably in years. Gorbachev never did muster the courage to initiate real economic change. Later in the year, he briefly endorsed a radical plan that would have dismantled the centralized communist economy and laid the foundation for a market system. But under pressure from hard-liners, he quickly backed down.

Endless dithering on Gorbachev's part, however, was becoming a less tenable option. The men who eventually led the coup against him were apoplectic over the disintegration of the Soviet Union. On the other end of the political spectrum, the populist politician, Boris N. Yeltsin, was zooming to prominence, his trajectory putting him on a collision course with both Gorbachev and the conservatives. In May 1990, the Russian parliament elected Yeltsin as its chairman, effectively making him president. After the vote, a horde of reporters followed Yeltsin as he went to meet the public. Scurrying across the inner courtyard of the Kremlin, Yeltsin and his entourage burst through the Spassky Gate, strode across Red Square, and slowed down beneath the multicolored onion domes of St. Basil's Cathedral. I watched as scores of Russians ran toward the burly, white-haired Yeltsin. Men grabbed his hands and patted him on the back. Women kissed him and thrust carnations and roses upon him. Beaming, Yeltsin moved to some nearby steps, clasped his hands over his head, and acknowledged the cheers—and hopes—of the crowd.

"Victory! Victory! Victory!" they chanted.

The year ended with the resignation of Gorbachev's close ally, Foreign Minister Eduard Shevardnadze, who stood before hundreds of stunned members of the Congress of People's Deputies and warned that the hard-liners were counterattacking and a "dictatorship was on the offensive." Several weeks later, as the final year of the Soviet Union began, Shevardnadze's prediction came to pass. Once again, the scene of the action was Lithuania. Soviet Army and KGB troops began occupying government buildings in an effort to regain control over the republic. Early on the morning of Sunday, January 13, I was where foreign correspondents were inclined to congregate after a 16-hour day of reporting and filing stories—in the bar of the Hotel Lithuania. I had scarcely consumed a beer when the phone in the bar rang, and someone reported that Soviet tanks and armored personnel carriers were heading for the city's TV tower. The press corps piled into cars and taxis, and, as we turned onto the road leading to the tower, we met the armored convoy. A military truck announced over a loudspeaker that a "Committee of National Salvation" was taking power in the republic. Suddenly, one of the tanks fired a shot—a blank, it turned out—and I was rocked by the blast that shattered the windows of nearby apartments. The tanks rolled over cars and pushed aside buses, shooting blanks as they went. I heard automatic-weapons fire just ahead, where a thousand Lithuanians stood guard around the tower. Sprinting ahead, trying to avoid being run over, I looked to my left just as a crowd of men ran up to a moving tank and tried to block its path. Lurching forward, the tank crushed one of the men to death.

At the tower, the troops cleared a way through the crowd by tossing stun grenades, beating people with their machine guns, and shooting the fiercest resisters. I saw a person, apparently dead, on the ground 20 yards away and heard, inside the tower, explosions and bursts of automatic-weapons fire as the troops occupied the building. At least 13 people were killed that night, and for the next several days Lithuanians waited for an attack on their parliament building, where hundreds of defenders had barricaded themselves inside. But the assault never came, and the attempted Soviet coup fizzled as the independent Lithuanian government remained in power, surrounded by hostile Soviet garrisons.

Gorbachev, facing harsh criticism from the West, realized his troops had gone too far. He had no stomach for shedding more blood.

For much of the rest of 1991, the U.S.S.R. felt, at best, as if it were stuck in neutral, and at worst as if it were sliding backward. In the Kremlin a fierce struggle over the direction of perestroika was being waged. Squeezed by reformers who wanted to continue moving ahead and reactionaries prophesying doom, Gorbachev seemed paralyzed and exhausted.

FOR AN AMERICAN BABY BOOMER, the Soviet Union was a revelation, and an inspiration. Nearly every day I was reminded how utterly pampered we were and how tough were the Soviets, who had lost 27 million people in World War II and probably that many in other 20th-century tragedies, such as World War I and Stalin's repressions. In Leningrad, I spent an afternoon with 77-year-old Maria Ivanovna Gustova, who had survived the 900-day Nazi siege of the city in the same communal apartment where we met. She had eaten leather and furniture glue, watched her mother starve to death,

and lost her 5-year-old son to dysentery. I wrote about her because she was one of the first, during those days of perestroika, to receive food packages from her former enemies, the Germans, who, a half century after the siege, were helping elderly Soviets during a difficult time. Gustova harbored no ill will toward the Germans, and was thankful for her tea, cookies, candy, and other delicacies.

A few months later, I profiled one of the U.S.S.R.'s first private farmers, Viktor Chumak, a potbellied, chain-smoking, 200-pound dynamo, who against absurd odds had acquired 1,600 acres, 100 head of cattle, 12 tractors, 2 harvesters, and 3 trucks. Operating under fledgling laws allowing limited business activities, Chumak had leased land from nearby collective farms, rented tractors, and purchased cattle using loans and savings. He displayed grit and good cheer, telling me, "We're in the Stone Age compared to the West. I feel like I'm building a house from scratch."

As the summer of 1991 began, events moved toward a climax more quickly than anyone anticipated. In early June, the people of Russia, for the first time in their thousand-year history, went to the polls to elect a leader. They chose Boris Yeltsin, who, as the popularly elected head of the massive Russian Republic, enjoyed a legitimacy that even Gorbachev—selected by the Politburo and the Congress of People's Deputies—could not claim. Yeltsin's victory created an increasingly untenable situation in which Gorbachev was at the helm of the Soviet Union, while Yeltsin was in charge of its Russian heartland. Soviet hard-liners quickly comprehended the threat Yeltsin posed, and shortly after his election three of the staunchest communist true believers—KGB chief Vladimir Kryuchkov, Defense Minister Dmitri Yazov, and Interior Minister Boris Pugo—spoke at a closed session of the Supreme Soviet and warned that perestroika was leading to the demise of the party and the dissolution of the Soviet Union.

On Monday, August 19, at 6:30 a.m., the telephone rang in our apartment. It was our upstairs neighbor and close friend, Lisa Dobbs, whose husband was bureau chief for the *Washington Post*. A friend of Michael's had just called, she said. The radio was announcing that a committee for state emergency had taken power from Mikhail Gorbachev. It was a hard-line coup. I sprinted to my office, two blocks away. It was not yet 11 p.m. in Philadelphia. I still had time to file a story.

It was a fine morning—warm, the sun well above the horizon, a few white clouds drifting across a blue sky—and it seemed incongruous that such an act would be unfolding on so sublime a day. But the clattering TASS machine confirmed that the Soviet Union's six-year experiment with democracy was apparently coming to an abrupt halt. The committee for state emergency, composed of most of the top men in Gorbachev's government—his vice president, prime minister, defense minister, KGB director, and chief of the armed forces—announced that they were seizing power because the leader's reforms had hit a dead end and were plunging the country "into the quagmire of violence and lawlessness." Gorbachev, they announced, was ill at his dacha in the Crimea.

Keeping the phone line open to my foreign desk, I repeatedly ran outside to look for signs of a military takeover. At first, it seemed like a normal summer morning, the streets quiet, a smattering of Muscovites heading for work. Soon, however, the columns of tanks and armored personnel carriers began to roll down Kutuzovsky Prospect, the wide avenue on which I lived. Around 9 a.m., my driver and I toured downtown Moscow. Troops were taking up positions in front of City Hall, the Kremlin, and the Ostankino TV tower. Some people were scared, some scornful, some merely incredulous. Did the staunch communists surrounding Gorbachev really think they could turn back the clock?

By late morning, I was at the Russian White House, the modern, high-rise, white-stone building that was the governmental seat of the Russian Republic and was fast becoming the center of resistance to the coup. Guards ushered me into the parliament's chambers, where Boris Yeltsin soon announced to the assembled reporters, diplomats, and Russian officials that he was leading the resistance to the communist takeover. As he spoke, someone informed him that tanks were encircling the building. Yeltsin wrapped up his remarks and marched outside, where an armored column was indeed moving into position on the road between the White House and the Moscow River. Yeltsin headed straight for them, acknowledging the cheers of a few dozen people before hopping onto one of the tanks.

"Citizens of Russia," he announced, reading from a piece of paper, "We are dealing with a right-wing, reactionary, anticonstitutional coup d'état.... We appeal to citizens of Russia to give an appropriate rebuff to the putschists and demand a return of the country to normal constitutional development."

It was Yeltsin's finest moment and the enduring image of the coup. Standing 15 feet from the president, my stomach knotted from excitement and fear. The young tank crew seemed flummoxed and uninterested in raising a hand against fellow Russians.

For me, the next three days were a sleepless, adrenaline-fueled marathon. The troops were tense at first but soon softened, as women gave them food and implored them not to obey the orders of the coup leaders. My wife, who is also a journalist, talked to many soldiers that Monday afternoon and came away convinced that the takeover was doomed. But I was not so sanguine. The crackdown in Lithuania was still fresh in my mind, and as thousands of people rallied to defend the White House, I feared that the junta might attempt an assault.

Our apartment was located only a few hundred yards from the White House, and armored personnel carriers formed a long queue along our avenue. Some of the stranger moments came when I dashed home for a meal, and, leaving the army columns on the street, walked into our compound. There, I found my daughters, aged two and one, on the playground with our Russian nanny, oblivious to the momentous events unfolding around them.

The coup's most sinister hour came late Tuesday night and early

Wednesday. By then, thousands of people, most of them unarmed, had thrown up a human shield around Yeltsin and the White House. It was raining, and the mood among the defenders was defiant, almost cocky. A rumor swept the crowd that armored columns were closing in on the White House from several directions. Around midnight, a fusillade of shots rang out as some protesters attacked a small armored convoy a few hundred yards away; three civilians died in the clash. Despite the tension, none of us realized then that the coup had, in effect, already collapsed. Elite KGB troops had refused to storm the White House. No one, not even the coup leaders, several of whom had been drunk throughout the crisis, had the resolve to spill the requisite blood.

On Wednesday, under sunny skies, the emergency committee called it quits, troops withdrew, and thousands of jubilant Russians streamed through the city. A crowd at Lubyanka Square shook their fists at KGB headquarters and prepared to tear down the statue of Feliks Dzerzhinsky, founder of the Soviet Secret Police. What everyone had feared, an attempt to yank Russia back to its totalitarian past, had taken place and been rebuffed, thanks in large part to Boris Yeltsin. The reactionaries who had tried to preserve the Soviet Union had succeeded, in 60 hours, in destroying it.

IT TOOK FOUR MORE MONTHS TO BURY the U.S.S.R. officially. In the fall of 1991, Gorbachev soon discovered that there was no more union over which to preside. With the republics on the periphery of the Soviet Union—along the Baltic, in the Caucasus, and in Central Asia—clearly wanting independence, Gorbachev tried in vain to preserve a union of Russia, Byelorussia, and Ukraine.

For Gorbachev and the U.S.S.R., the end came on December 25, 1991. I had spent Christmas day at our dacha, 25 miles from Moscow, a picturesque spot where I would cross-country ski for hours through pine and birch forests. After a Christmas lunch with family and friends, I drove back to the capital to watch Gorbachev deliver a terse resignation speech, in which he lamented the disintegration of the Soviet Union but praised the people for helping him dismantle the totalitarian communist state. I felt a wave of sympathy for the Soviet leader, who had tried so hard to bend history to his will, only to find he could not control the forces he had unleashed. Eager to reform the Soviet Union, he wound up presiding over its demise, a fact that haunted him.

Many Russians scorned him as pompous, verbose, and indecisive. Others gave him his due. "He broke the customary way of life for generations of Soviets," wrote journalist Yuri Shekoschikin. "He did what would have been death to his predecessors—he eliminated the distance between the leader and his subjects. Maybe that was deadly for his welfare in this land of slaves. He was criticized—timidly at first by people who took pride in their boldness and were amazed that no police cars appeared beneath their windows, then more confidently, boldly, forcefully.... He made a lot of mistakes, but why do we take his errors more emotionally than his predecessors? Maybe because it was *us* he freed. Oh, are we going to remember him."

That night around 8 p.m., I went to Red Square. An hour earlier, guards had struck the red hammer-and-sickle flag that flew over the Kremlin and replaced it with Russia's red-, blue-, and-white tricolor. I had half expected crowds, perhaps even a celebration, but only a few dozen people were walking around the vast, cobblestoned square. It was spitting snow, and the scene was remarkable only for the pervasive sense of anticlimax. Even I, an outsider, was nearly numb from watching two years of history unfold. For the Russians, the fatigue of being buffeted by great events was far more profound.

But many Russians also felt hope that night. The communists had been routed. Yeltsin was in charge. Capitalism was on its way. After seven decades of Soviet rule and six tumultuous years of perestroika, people were cautiously optimistic that they might at last get a glimpse of the shining future that had long been dangled before them. ■

DONETSK,

UKRAINE 1992

After a day in the pits, a coal

miner scrubs down. Though

relatively well paid, miners face

equipment breakdowns and gas

explosions as they extract

Ukraine's high-grade coal. Every

million tons costs the life of one

miner, according to estimates—

a figure ten times higher than

comparable U.S. fatality rates.

ALMATY,

KAZAKHSTAN 1992

At the central market on a

Sunday morning, vendors sell

everything from furniture and

shoes to livestock and produce.

MOSCOW 1992

*Blindfolded by a child, a
statue of Stalin, most feared
ruler of the communist era, sits
amid other toppled effigies of
party leaders now jumbled
together in a Moscow park. To
ardent believers in the glories
of communism, such disrespect
is heresy. To hopeful new
democrats, the jigsaw jumble
signifies freedom.*

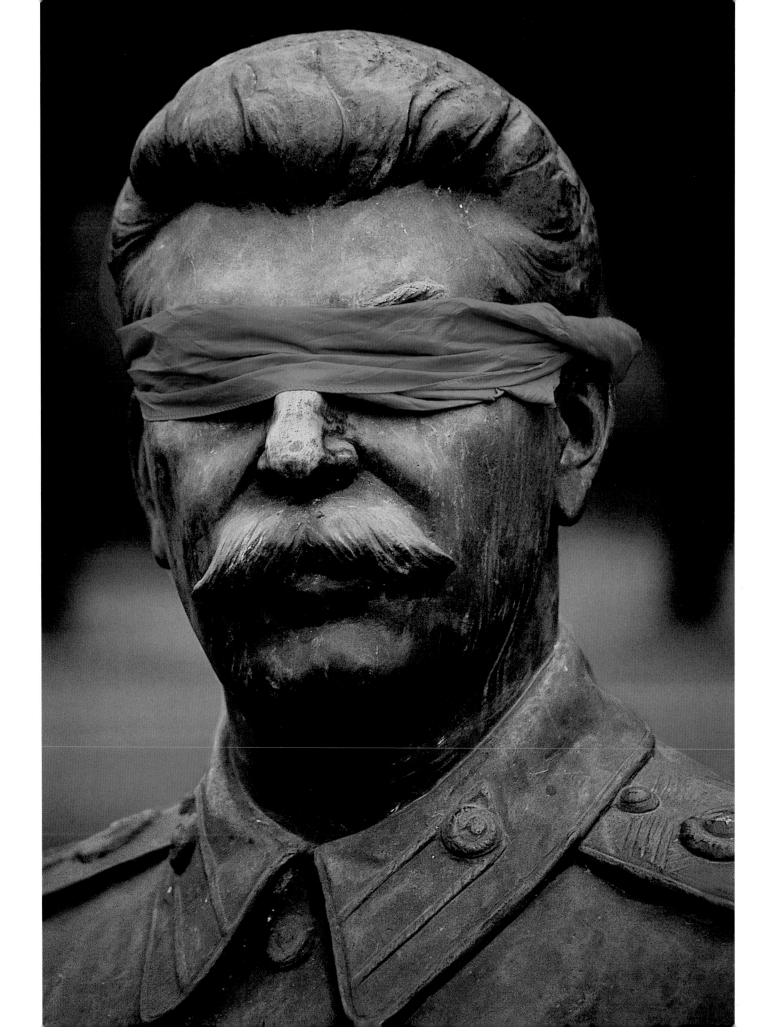

MOSCOW 1996

Retirees like this couple—he

a former accountant and she

a scientist—are among those

least able to adapt to the new

economy. Skyrocketing prices

strain their modest pensions,

which combined equal about

half the current average wage.

MOSCOW 1991

*Like this Muscovite, many of
Russia's elderly live in poorly
maintained, communal flats,
where they are forced to share
kitchens and bathrooms.*

MOSCOW 1996

On International Labor Day,

disgruntled Russians demand a

return to communism,

preferable, in their minds, to

the uncertainties of the current

economy, the omnipresence of

the mafia, and the perceived

corruption of politicians.

MOSCOW 1996

*Monument to history, Red
Square perpetually anchors
Moscow to its past, no matter
the changing times. Crouched
beneath the ornate spires
of the Kremlin towers, erected
during the long tenure of the
tsars, is the stark Socialist
pyramid housing Lenin's
mausoleum—reminder of a
recent, if comparatively brief,
experiment that failed.*

UKRAINE 1992

Along a highway near Kiev, where gas is dear and vodka plentiful, a stranded motorist offers one for the other. As Ukrainians struggle to adjust to a market economy, many resort to barter to survive.

MOSCOW 1993

Hoping for a little pocket

change, a young Muscovite

cleans the windshields of

passing motorists. Most drivers,

wary of thieves, remove wiper

blades and reattach them only

when it rains.

MOSCOW 1992

In Lubyanskaya Square,

a babushka finds her own

niche in the new economy.

Peddling goods on the street

became legal, briefly, in 1992.

But the impromptu tolkuchi,

or "push markets," created

so much street congestion that

they were soon restricted.

MOSCOW 1992

Jobless and homeless: In the early 1990s, the homeless became a feature of Moscow street life. This man was evicted from his apartment by his own son, who decided he needed the space for his live-in girlfriend.

**VLADIMIR,
RUSSIA 1992**

A bread-and-butter breakfast might not be much, but at least prisoners in the Vladimir penitentiary can count on a steady flow of food. On the "outside," people go hungry as food prices spiral.

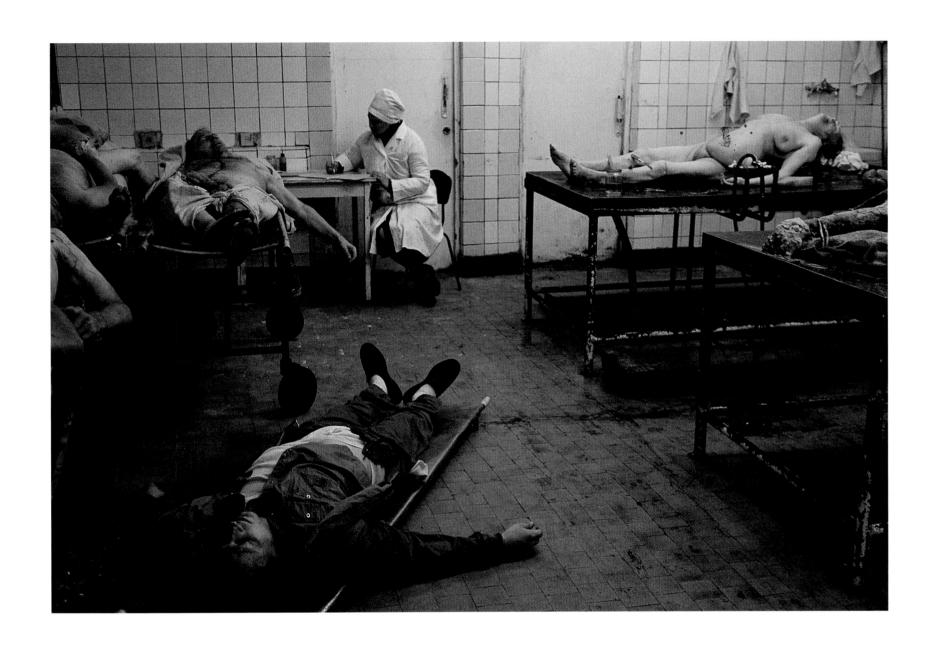

KIEV, UKRAINE 1992

Even Ukraine's morgues reflect

the state of the country's

economy—though this one

was cleaned up before the

photographer arrived. Bodies

often go unclaimed because

relatives can't afford a funeral.

KIEV, UKRAINE 1992

Young devotees of Kiev's underground art scene openly share marijuana grown in backyard gardens. Such drug use was extremely rare in Soviet times.

BERLIN, GERMANY 1996

In a mocking tribute to the

past, this "portrait" of former

Soviet Premier Leonid

Brezhnev and former East

German leader Erich Honecker

adorns a remaining stretch of

the Berlin Wall.

**NOVOKUZNETSK,
RUSSIA 1992**

*Smoke from the KMK steel
plant belches carbon monoxide
above this Siberian city. By the
early 1990s, pollution had
impacted every major river in
Russia, had left one quarter of
the drinking water unsafe, and
had cursed 35 million Russians
with unhealthy air.*

KUNDA, ESTONIA 1993

*Workers take welcome breaths
after a shift in the dust-filled
confines of their cement plant.
Exposure to the pollution leaves
them exhausted at day's end.*

CHELYABINSK,
RUSSIA 1993

*New housing rising in the
shadow of highly polluting
metallurgical and energy plants
threatens to create additional
problems for this Ural city,
also afflicted by the aftermath
of nearby nuclear accidents.*

PROKOPYEVSK,

RUSSIA 1993

Mineral wealth has lead to ill

health and soot-caked snow

in Siberia's industrial-rich

Kuzbas region. Respiratory

and other diseases are on the

increase here, particularly

among the area's most

vulnerable inhabitants.

65

SHYMKENT,

KAZAKHSTAN 1992

Proud of its product, an

automotive plant displays one

of its models. This city in

southern Kazakhstan supports

itself on heavy industry.

DONETSK,

UKRAINE 1992

Heavy smoking only increases

the risk of lung cancer and

other bronchial diseases among

miners, whose jobs ensure a

daily diet of coal dust.

VOLGOGRAD,

RUSSIA 1992

In the mid-1980s, some 300
tractors daily rolled off this
factory's assembly line.
Hampered by machinery
dating from the 1930s, some
workers still produce tractors,
while others have started to
make freezers for soft ice cream.

NOVOKUZNETSK,

RUSSIA 1993

At the KMK steel plant, one

of Siberia's oldest, employees

take tea and warm themselves

between firings of the plant's

open-hearth furnaces.

MAGNITOGORSK,

RUSSIA 1993

On winter weekends, men drill

fishing holes in the thick ice

of the Ural River to try their

luck. Knowing that the river is

badly polluted by waste from

the Lenin Steel Works looming

behind them, they often sell

their catch to markets rather

than consume it themselves.

ARAL SEA,

KAZAKHSTAN 1993

Walking on water, metaphori-

cally, camels cross the dry bed

of the Aral Sea. Irrigation

tapping into the lake's feeder

rivers has shrunk its size by

half and created this graveyard

of rusting shipwrecks, where

once a beautiful bay glistened.

MOSCOW 1992

A postcard-perfect view of Red Square rescued from a trash pile strikes an ironic note as people search the garbage dump for more utilitarian items, like food, bottles, and construction materials.

MOSCOW 1996

With prices rising and wages

often delayed by months, some

Russians have been forced to

scavenge local trash bins

to survive.

ELISTA, RUSSIA 1991

Considered a purveyor of fine viands, the Elista Meat Plant puts out over 13,000 tons of beef, pork, horse, lamb, and camel meat each year.

MOSCOW 1991

At a bakery, a shopkeeper awaits customers in the dawn of capitalism. Accustomed to subsidized food, Russians were shocked when eggs, bread, butter, and milk prices began to follow market trends instead of government regulation.

MOSCOW 1991

*In the early 1990s, 70-some
soup kitchens welcomed poor
Muscovites unable to cope on
their own with the exhorbitant
rise in food costs.*

BAKU,

AZERBAIJAN 1993

A gloss of oil and chemicals

sheens standing water in an

oil field near Baku. Runoff

from these fields has rendered

local streams, lakes, and ponds

biologically dead.

MOSCOW 1993

Unsolved tragedy: These children, all from only two neighborhoods in Moscow, were born with missing forearms. Although no certain links can be drawn between their defects and Moscow's bewildering mix of pollutants, the incidence of congenital deformities is higher here than in the rest of Russia.

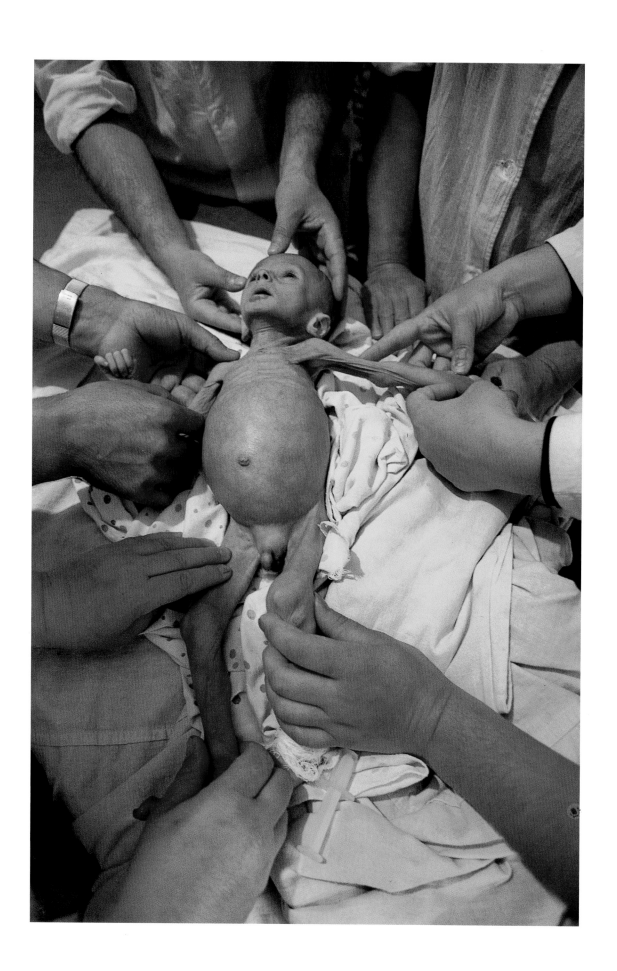

SUMQAYIT,

AZERBAIJAN 1993

Deadly heritage: Hospital staff care for a five-month-old boy plagued by immune deficiencies. An hour after this picture was taken, the young patient unexpectedly succumbed to his ailments. Pollution from chemical plants has afflicted the immune systems of many children and pregnant women.

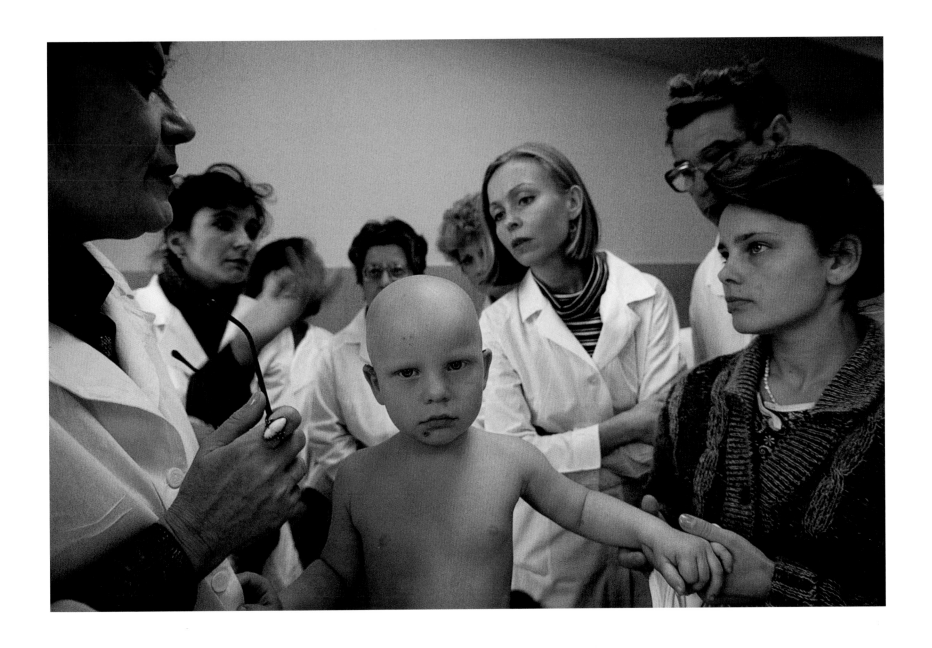

KIEV, UKRAINE 1993

Baffling cases of baldness in children have doctors worried in the Ukraine, where a dramatic increase in thyroid cancer among the young has been attributed to radiation from the 1986 disaster at the Chornobyl nuclear plant.

BAKU,

AZERBAIJAN 1993

Strange playground: Children

cavort in the inky pools of

runoff from leaking oil pumps.

Azerbaijan's fields lost promi-

nence when oil exploration

shifted to Siberia in the

1960s, but they have since

made a comeback.

MUSLYUMOVO,
RUSSIA 1993

*Cattle graze and children
play on meadows along the
Techa River, ignoring the high
contamination here from
careless dumping and major
accidents in a nearby weapons
plutonium plant.*

88

SEMEY,

KAZAKHSTAN 1993

Nuclear fallout from the
Semey test site has resulted in a
plague of birth defects among the
children of northeastern
Kazakhstan. Now 13, this boy,
who actually lives on the test site,
was born blind and disfigured.

PRYPYAT,

UKRAINE 1993

Desolation blows through the town of Prypyat, a city built for the workers of the ill-fated Chornobyl power complex. On April 26, 1986, the world's worst nuclear accident contaminated thousands of square miles in this area, displacing some 150,000 people.

KUPUVATE,
UKRAINE 1993

The apple may be "hot" and the cow's milk contaminated, but for two aged returnees to the village of Kupuvate, it's worth the risk to be home. So far, some 700 evacuees— most elderly women—have returned to the area impacted by Chornobyl.

KIEV, UKRAINE 1993

Chornobyl invalids line up

to register in Kiev. Their "degree

of victimhood"—one through

four—will determine the

compensation awarded them.

TWO A WINDOW OPENS

In the first week of January 1992, just a few days after the demise of the U.S.S.R., capitalism flattened Russia. Free markets begin with free prices, and the initial step taken by Boris Yeltsin's economic wunderkinder was to liberate the cost of goods, which hadn't changed much in decades. The Yeltsin team called their overhaul "shock therapy." It was an apt phrase. On January 2, 1992, the government declared that most prices should seek their own levels. They quickly did, shooting up three, five, even ten times; wages and pensions only doubled or tripled. Overnight, tens of millions of Russians became impoverished, their savings rendered virtually worthless.

The story was not hard to cover. Indeed, walking out my door, I literally tripped over it. By the second week of January, Moscow's sidewalks were crowded with long lines of people, mainly elderly, selling everything from family porcelain and jewelry to pickles, cigarettes, and perfume. Standing in subzero temperatures, these peddlers were the first wave of what would become a flood of street capitalists—Russians struggling to survive. Within weeks, kiosks began sprouting up on sidewalks all over the capital, their owners hoping to make a quick profit selling candy bars, beer, panty hose, and dozens of other items. Within months, a new breed of Russian, known as the "shuttle trader," appeared. Engineers, teachers, factory workers and other middle-class Russians who had lost their jobs or who hadn't been paid in ages, the shuttle traders traveled to countries like Turkey and India, bought cheap goods, and, burdened with enormous bundles, returned to Russia to peddle their wares on the street.

Many Russians were in a state of shock, chagrined that the move to a market system looked more like a squalid Levantine bazaar than the well-oiled capitalist machine of their dreams. As austere as life had been under the old regime, it had guaranteed Soviets one thing: security. Now, in a flash, that immunity from hunger and poverty seemed to have evaporated.

"It's an outrage," Klara Shestakova, 61, a retiree and onetime Yeltsin supporter told me on a bitter cold January afternoon as she stood with 200 people proffering goods on Moscow's Leninsky Prospect. "I worked for 30 years as an engineer, and now I am forced to stand here and sell things to survive. How this will all end I have no idea…. I don't believe in anyone anymore." For those of us in the foreign press corps, a story that had been stirring and crystal clear—good-guy reformers and Soviet masses vanquish Bolshevik dinosaurs—quickly became murky and anything but inspirational. Boris Yeltsin sometimes dropped out of sight for days, occasionally reappearing in a decidedly unsober state. His economic reforms began to look hasty and ill conceived, involving far more destruction of the old than creation of the new. One Russian friend compared the 1992 economic revolution to a man gleefully razing his dilapidated shack without giving any thought to what he might build in its place.

Still, despite the mounting hardships, most Russian reformers and western experts supported Yeltsin's plunge into capitalism, led by Yegor Gaidar, the 35-year-old economic czar. Seven decades of the Soviet-planned economy, they reasoned, could not be undone without considerable pain. I was of the same opinion and embraced the notion that turning a communist economy into a capitalist one was a daunting task, a bit like trying to put a scrambled egg back in its shell. By the spring of 1992, after more than two years in the former Soviet Union, I knew that Russia was a sprawling, unruly place with little history of democracy or a market system. Still, I thought—quite naively, it turned out—that our American system could be more or less grafted onto Russia. How wrong I was. I, and many others, grossly underestimated the enormous drag that Russia's history, both prerevolutionary and communist, would have on the reform effort. A centuries-old tradition of corruption and bribe-taking merged with the prevailing ethos of the late Soviet era (rip off the state, because the state is screwing you) to pervert many of Yeltsin's reforms. Shackled for 70 years, Russia, which had never had a civil, democratic society, went wild in the capitalist era, with the spoils going to the well connected and the new Russian mafiosi. I had many misapprehensions about the Russian character, one of which was straightened out by the poet Yevgeny Yevtushenko when I talked with him at a reception. At one point I commented on the passivity of the Russian people, to which the writer replied, "My dear, you don't understand Russians at all. We are anarchists to our bones."

THE WINTER OF 1992 seemed endless. After glimpsing the sun only a couple of times in a month, one colleague likened living in Moscow in winter to being underwater; all was grayness and murk. In May, however, spring finally arrived with fresh breezes and brilliant sun. One Saturday in late May I drove west out of town, crossed Moscow's beltway, the Ring Road, and immediately entered a 19th-century rural Russia of log cabins, forests, and fields. Soon enough, aping the American suburban dream, the nouveau riche would begin erecting gaudy manses here, ruining the charm of the capital's once rustic environs.

That afternoon, it seemed that Moscow's entire population had migrated to the countryside and was planting potatoes in the moist, dark earth. Thanks to communism, Russia was saddled with a woeful system of collective agriculture, but the Russians themselves had some of the greenest thumbs in the world. After five months of market-induced trauma, no one was taking any chances. Their faith in the state having gone up in smoke, Russians were learning to rely solely on themselves for survival, and they headed en masse to the fields to secure a supply of potatoes, carrots, onions, and pickled cucumbers for the coming winter. I stepped out of my car near a field where dozens of people were planting. Apple trees blossomed against a bright blue sky and a cuckoo sang in a stand of birches. One man, 25-year-old Alexander Kuznetsov, was seeding potatoes with his brothers, their wives, and his mother and father in a 60-by-100-foot plot. Their crop of vegetables, together with the family's pigs and 80 chickens, would ensure the clan's survival, no matter what the Yeltsin economic team threw their way.

"I'm not just going to lie down here and give up and die," Kuznetsov said. "We count only on ourselves, and that's why we're out here today.... Look at this land. I'd love to work it my whole life. You know, if we only had a decent system, we'd be the ones sending you humanitarian aid."

Not everyone was as enthusiastic as Kuznetsov. Nearby, a middle-aged woman in a head scarf, Lyubov Kondrashova, was pulling weeds in her potato plot. She quickly let me know she'd rather be spending her Saturday elsewhere. "It's one thing to come out here if you get pleasure out of it," she said. "But it's quite another thing if you're out here because you know that, if you don't plant, you'll be left sucking your fingers next winter, because there's nothing to eat."

All was not bleak, however, in the first years of Russia's transition to the market. In Moscow and in the provinces, many stores began to appear, with the likes of Benetton, Yves Rocher perfumes, and Dannon foods opening in the capital. Though unsightly, the plethora of street kiosks and peddlers was a sign that Russians did, indeed, possess capitalist instincts. And no one could deny that a previously unimaginable array of goods and food was for sale; the hallmark of the Soviet economy—scarcity and lines—had disappeared. Russians quipped that now they had everything, except money. Opinions about the country's transition to capitalism tended to split along generational lines, with the young excited about the possibilities and many middle-aged and elderly angry over the seemingly heedless rush to the market and the precipitous drop in the standard of living.

By the early spring of 1992, the backlash to the reforms had gathered momentum and become the defining political struggle in the country. Allies who had stood with Yeltsin during the August 1991 coup, including Vice President Alexander Rutskoi, turned against the Russian president, accusing his economic brain trust of slavishly mimicking the West at the expense of the Russian people. By early 1993, Russia was split by a fierce political struggle, with the parliamentary opposition nearly impeaching Yeltsin. The ire of communist and hard-line lawmakers was further fueled by the government's most ambitious reform, the privatization process, during which the government sold shares in state-run businesses and industry to workers, management, and investors. Privatization was a vital step, but the process was riddled with corruption and insider dealing that often left workers with little or nothing.

In 1993, I visited the Vladimir Tractor Factory, a shabby, slogan-covered giant redolent of the old Soviet Union. The aging brick plant, which employed 18,000 people, was crammed with outmoded equipment. The air was smoky, the metal floors slick with oil, and the tractors that rolled off the assembly line looked like vintage 1960s. Some of the employees, who were to purchase 51 percent of the shares in the plant, were excited about the prospect of owning the factory. But others, such as 51-year-old Vladimir Vlasov, were worried that factory directors, the mafia, or foreign investors would actually wind up controlling the plant and plundering its assets.

(Vlasov's fears frequently came to pass. In some instances, managers illegally grabbed enterprises. In others, workers unloaded shares, or vouchers, perceived as worthless. Both scenarios allowed unscrupulous owners to take control of factories.)

"People are not ready for privatization. It has happened so suddenly that no one has had a chance to figure out what it means," Vlasov told me. "People have been deceived so many times before by their government, and I'm afraid that this will turn out to be just another deception."

My tour as Moscow correspondent of the *Philadelphia Inquirer* ended in May 1993. On May 1, as I was preparing to leave, mobs of disgruntled workers—organized by Yeltsin's opponents—led a violent demonstration in Moscow in which a policeman was killed. It was a bad omen. Over the next two years, as my newspaper sent me back to Russia during times of crisis, my arrival was often accompanied by the sound of gunfire.

FIVE MONTHS LATER, on October 4, 1993, I landed at Sheremetyevo Airport as Russian tanks were shelling the White House, ground zero in the resistance to the August 1991 coup. Yeltsin had disbanded the Russian parliament that had tried to impeach him, and for two weeks a group of hard-line lawmakers and their allies had been holed up inside the modern, 20-story White House. On Sunday, October 3, in what amounted to a second coup, Yeltsin's opponents had attempted to seize power, storming the state TV tower and setting off a gun battle that killed a dozen people. The next day, Yeltsin ordered an assault on the mutineers in the White House. In the center of the capital, firing from a bridge spanning the Moscow River, tanks blasted the building, after which troops stormed the stronghold. Over a hundred people died in the attack and related clashes. My driver sped in from the airport, dropping me in my old neighborhood a few blocks from the White House. Running down Kutuzovsky Prospect, I heard the sound of machine-gun fire. Soon I saw the Russian government building, most of its windows blown out and smoke pouring from numerous floors. Standing in the street and on nearby rooftops, several thousand onlookers watched as Yeltsin's troops took the White House. That night, sniper fire echoed down the wide avenues where I used to push my daughters in baby strollers.

Fourteen months later, at the end of 1994, I was back in Russia again, this time to cover far worse fighting. The Caucasus territory of Chechnya had declared its independence, and, Yeltsin, believing generals who boasted that their troops could take the capital in 48 hours, sent the army to subdue the Chechens. On December 31, I arrived at the border of Chechnya and Dagestan, bivouacking in the town of Khasavyurt. That day, New Year's Eve, Russian troops stormed Grozny, the Chechen capital. Conflicting reports filtered back to Khasavyurt, within 50 miles of Grozny, and on January 1, 1995, I hired a taxi to take me to the battle zone. My driver was a slight, mustachioed, affable man in his mid-40s, and, as we rode out of Khasavyurt, he muttered prayers to Allah as I silently made my own entreaties to the Almighty. I had managed to secure a bullet-proof vest for the driver and was wearing a vest and helmet myself. It was cold and foggy in Chechnya, and, as we sped down the largely deserted roads, we expressed our relief over the gloomy weather, which would keep Russian war planes from spotting us. The driver was cautious and edgy, traits I was happy to see; I did not want my fate in the hands of a hot dog.

As we approached a traffic circle and prepared to drive the last leg into Grozny, I expected to see beleaguered Chechen fighters fleeing the capital. Instead, hundreds of young, bearded Chechens, many shouting "God is Great," headed into the city on the backs of trucks, firing their guns in the air in celebration. The Russians, they proclaimed, had been routed.

We sped into Grozny, the sound of artillery and automatic-weapons fire intensifying as we neared the center. Finally, we reached a street teeming with fighters, some carrying rocket-propelled grenades, others wrapped in bandoliers of ammunition. The shooting was intense only a few hundred yards away; one fighter warned us not to go any farther. Just then an artillery shell crashed into the next block. I needed no more convincing to stay put.

I roamed the street, talking to a dozen men who had participated in the battle the night before. They all described the same scene: Russian tanks and armored personnel carriers had poured into Grozny, where the Chechens had quickly disabled the vehicles with handheld, antitank rockets and Molotov cocktails. The rebels then shot the Russian troops as they scrambled out of the burning armor. "Allah was with us," declared Mavlad Akhmatov, who said his squad destroyed two tanks and two armored personnel carriers. "I will not take any prisoners. Now, God willing, we will chase the Russians all the way to the Volga."

The accounts of the Chechen fighters turned out to be true. The Russian New Year's Eve assault was a debacle in which dozens of armored vehicles had been destroyed and hundreds of soldiers, most of them inexperienced, killed. I filled up my notebook, trying hard not to flinch every time a shell crashed into nearby blocks. "That's it!" I told the driver as I finished my last interview, and we hustled to our car and drove away. As we left Grozny and hit the open road to Khasavyurt, my relief at fleeing the city was indescribable.

I spent ten more days in Chechnya and came away convinced that, like the American troops in Vietnam, the Russians had no hope of subduing the Chechens. I had witnessed the start of a conflict that continues to drain Russia to this day. For me, the most surreal moment in Chechnya came on January 5 in Grozny, as I drove down Lenin Street after witnessing fighting near the presidential palace. The city was fast being pounded into ruin, and Lenin Street presented a grim tableau: gas mains burning, buildings scarred by shell fragments and bullets, power lines dangling, burned out Russian armored vehicles littering the roadway. As we sped out of town, I saw three Russian babushkas standing in front of a solid, five-story stucco building. I asked the driver to stop, and I approached one of the women. She took my hand and said, "Come with me." She then led me into the basement, down passageways as black as coal, and into a warren of rooms where about a hundred people, most of them elderly, ethnic Russians, were living by candlelight in a Cold War bomb shelter. Unable to flee Grozny because they were too old, too sick, or didn't have relatives nearby, they were eking out an existence as Yeltsin's troops laid siege to the city.

"Oh, Yeltsin has sent us humanitarian aid—120 tons of bombs," said my guide, Lyuba Nalitova, as she nudged me deeper into the shelter.

I STAYED AWAY FROM RUSSIA for a year and a half. But the place still exerted a strong pull on me, and in July 1996 I returned to spend the summer and fall traveling overland across the country. I was writing a travel/adventure book and planned to fly-fish from the Norwegian border to the Pacific coast, meandering through what had always been my favorite part of Russia—its rural backwaters. I landed in Moscow on July 3, the day Boris Yeltsin defeated Communist Party candidate Gennady Zyuganov and was re-elected president. Most people were too weary to be euphoric, but there was a great sense of relief among reform-minded Russians, a feeling that, with Zyuganov's defeat, the country had crossed the Rubicon and could never return to its communist past. People were right about that, but Yeltsin's triumph also came at a high cost.

The campaign was a setback for the young free press, as many of Yeltsin's financial backers, who also controlled major television stations and newspapers, saw to it that the election coverage was absurdly one-sided. But far more damaging were the behind-the-scenes machinations that enabled a handful of businessmen, known as the oligarchs, to gain control of major segments of the economy in exchange for supporting Yeltsin. (Some of the oligarchs were well-connected former communists who cashed in on the privatization process, while others were simply shrewd businessmen who saw in the new Russia opportunities, such as trading in oil or opening car dealerships, and seized them.) Anatoly Chubais, the man in charge of Russia's privatization program, had permitted several of the oligarchs's banks, which had provided the government with much needed loans, to acquire large blocks of shares in huge industrial concerns through shady auctions. These insider deals enabled a few financial institutions to gain control over many major enterprises, such as Norilsk Nickel, at bargain-basement prices. To show their gratitude, the oligarchs contributed as much as $140 million to Yeltsin's re-election campaign. Chubais and Yeltsin justified their actions by saying they wanted to get as much of the economy into private hands as quickly as possible, making it nearly impossible for any future government to return to a centralized economy. Indeed, by the end of the privatization process, 70 percent of the country's economic production was generated by privately owned companies.

"They steal and steal and steal," Chubais said of the country's new capitalists. "They are stealing absolutely everything, and it is impossible to stop them. But let them steal and take their property. They will then become owners and decent administrators of this property."

The real problem, as author Chrystia Freeland pointed out in *Sale of the Century*, was that the Russian tycoons, enjoying the fruits of giant, monopolistic enterprises, had little incentive to restructure their businesses. Russia, Freeland noted, privatized its industries faster than other former Soviet states, but its economy has remained more sluggish than many because of rampant mismanagement and inefficiency.

In the countryside, a vast expanse that extended more than 5,000 miles across ten time zones, the average Russian was oblivious to such intrigue. With factories and collective farms either laying off workers or not paying wages for months at a time, the inhabitants of Russia's countryside were focused on their own survival. Russia was a nation turned on its head, a place that had, in just five years, gone from the shabby, secure embrace of the Soviet system to the disorder and insecurity of a perverse capitalist economy. From the window of the Trans-Siberian Railroad, Russia looked like one endless potato patch as people scrambled to support themselves. As I traveled, I was reminded of a Russian proverb that conveyed the sense of abandonment and isolation familiar to Russian peasants for centuries: "God is a long way up, and the Tsar is a long way off."

Early in my trip, I stopped in Serdobsk, about 300 miles southeast of Moscow, to see what had happened to Viktor Chumak, the private farmer I had written about five years earlier. From 1992 to 1994, with the help of a loan worth several hundred thousand dollars, Viktor had expanded his 1,600-acre spread to 4,000 acres and built a horse stable, a cattle shed, and a grain bin. But in 1995, interest rates shot up from 28 percent to 200 percent, and, unable to make his payments, Viktor lost nearly everything to the bank. His creditors left him two combines and a couple of trucks, and with this equipment Viktor was hanging on, tilling his own land and contracting his services to local collective farms. By the time I caught up with him, Chumak was a chastened man.

"You developed your capitalist markets in the West over hundreds of years, and our government wants our people to go to sleep one night in a communist world and wake up the next morning in a capitalist one," Viktor told me. "We're a long way from the market. We don't even know what the word means. We don't have a market. We have a fucking bazaar!"

I spent a few days with Viktor, and by the end it was clear that, despite his setbacks, he still had the energy and determination to hang on as a private farmer. When I joked that if things got much worse he would have to join a collective farm, Chumak shot back, "They wouldn't be able to produce enough vodka to console me if I were stuck on a collective farm." He told me that he had not forsaken his dream of rebuilding his operation and constructing a dairy and sausage-processing plant.

Leaving Chumak, I spent two months in Siberia, where conditions were harsher, people tougher, and the state a distant presence. My journey there was like time travel. Many rural Siberians lived in log huts, fetched their water from wells, cut their own wood for heating, and tended massive gardens. People often lived on a subsistence level, hunting and fishing to supplement what they grew themselves.

Near Lake Baikal, I fished with several men who had turned to sable trapping and meat hunting after being laid off by lumber mills and mining companies. Along the Barguzin River, which runs into Lake Baikal, trapper Valery Songolov told me that sable, fox, squirrel, and other animals were becoming scarce as poaching and illegal trapping grew. "We used to have 600 workers employed in this area with the forestry industry," he said. "Now they're all unemployed. They've got to live, so they head to the woods and kill what they can."

Nearly everywhere I went in Siberia, poaching was rampant, and I worried that Russia was depleting its stocks of wildlife and fish. But conservation is for people with full stomachs, and many Russians were too busy simply surviving to fret about the environment. Denizens of the former Soviet Union also tended to be more fatalistic, as I saw firsthand when I visited Chornobyl six years after the nuclear accident. There, a thousand people had illegally moved back to a highly contaminated zone within 18 miles of the reactor. The residents, most of them elderly, had missed their rustic cabins and the peaceful countryside surrounding Chornobyl. I met several women who ate mushrooms grown in the radioactive soil and drank milk from cows grazing on the polluted land. "I don't think we have radiation here—it just flew away to some other area," said Paraska Korovchenko, 73. "We're not afraid of radiation any longer."

As I traveled across Siberia in 1996, I came across shoots of private enterprise emerging from the ruins of the old system. Hitchhiking through Kolyma—a wild stretch of the Russian Far East that once was home to the deadliest camps in Stalin's gulag—I was inevitably picked up by long-haul truckers who were making out fine in the new Russia. Using one main road, they carried goods from China or Korea to the scattered towns of the area, traveling through a wild, beautiful landscape where golden larch trees covered low, rugged mountains. The men earned the equivalent of several thousand dollars a month—a princely sum in Russia – and were part of a tiny, emerging middle class. "Before we just earned kopecks," one trucker told me. "Now I can earn good money. There's no comparison."

I LEFT RUSSIA on October 11, more than a hundred days after I began my journey. My trip had not provided any startling revelations, but it had better enabled me to see the country as it was, not as I wanted it to be. As a correspondent during perestroika, I had viewed the titanic struggle in the Soviet Union as a kind of spectator sport. I cheered on Gorbachev and Yeltsin as they battled the Neandertals who wanted to preserve the communist past. I rooted for Yeltsin's economic whiz kids as they busted up the Soviet economy and began willy-nilly to privatize Russian industry. Wasn't it great that these bright young men were building a Slavic version of America?

I know now that I was a fool. As a naive American of limited vision, I failed to see that you couldn't simply impose capitalism on Russia. I didn't understand how corruption, inefficiency, and bureaucracy would make a mockery of many of the reforms. Yeltsin's brand of economic therapy seemed like a great idea—get the pain over quickly then move on to the shining capitalist future. But my journey had stripped me of my certainty; I had seen too much upheaval, too much poverty.

Few people, not even those at the center of the action in Russia, fully appreciated how much damage seven decades of communism had done, or how painful the country's rebirth would be. Anatoly Chubais put it well: "We...did not comprehend the enormity of the process we were dealing with. We thought it was a difficult transition that would last three years, five years, seven years. Now it's clear that it will last decades." ■

MOSCOW 1996

*GUM, the largest department
store in the country, offers
window shoppers a glimpse of
reflected Russian glory—the
Kremlin's towers and St. Basil
Cathedral. Its prime location
on Red Square has attracted
big international brands: Dior,
Lancôme, and Galleries
Lafayette have all vied to open
branches in this GUM store.*

VESHENSKAYA,

RUSSIA 1997

At the end of a long, hot day,

villagers retreat to the Don

River to water their livestock

and take a refreshing dip.

**NOVOCHERKASSK,
RUSSIA 1997**

*Following a proud tradition,
a young soldier-to-be is fitted
for his uniform at the Royal
Cossack Cadet Academy.
Established by Tsar Alexander
III in 1883, closed by Stalin
in 1933, the academy reopened
its doors in 1991.*

MOSCOW 1996

As the relentless Russian winter

recedes, grateful Muscovites

take to the streets again.

SIBERIA, RUSSIA 1997

World's longest railroad, the Trans-Siberian is a century-old monument to the tsars' imperial will, the Soviet Union's might, and Russia's resilience. From Moscow, it heads east through the Ural Mountains and across Asia to Vladivostok, on the Sea of Japan.

CROSSING

THE URALS 1996

A couple who met aboard the

Trans-Siberian savor a first-

class moment together.

**PETROVSKIY ZAVOD,
RUSSIA 1997**

*Taking advantage of a stop
on the long-distance rail line,
babushkas offer passengers
their home-cooked food and
garden produce, which they
cart to the station aboard
baby carriages.*

KRASNOYARSK,

RUSSIA 1997

In south-central Siberia, biting

cold frosts the windows of an

electrichka, *a local electric*

train, where a passenger sports

the classic Russian defense

against winter—a fur shapka.

**KRASNOYARSK,
RUSSIA 1997**

*Seemingly just another train
station, the Krasnoyarsk stop
also provides access to two
"secret" cities, unmarked on
Soviet-era maps because they
produced plutonium and
military electronics.*

MOSCOW 1992

Stealing a kiss good-bye in the

corridor of a train making its

way through Moscow

SVISHCHEVO,

RUSSIA 1992

As a train hurtles by, villagers

in the Siberian taiga take little

notice. Some who are carless

still rely on a time-honored

mode of transportation—

horse-drawn sleighs.

DIVNOMORSKOYE,

RUSSIA 1997

At first light, young Cossack

cadets are up. Though millions

of Cossacks were killed in

Stalin's purges, they have made

a mighty comeback, with

thousands of new recruits

joining their ranks.

NOVOCHERKASSK,

RUSSIA 1997

A Cossack soldier stands at

attention for a ceremony mark-

ing Russia's recognition of the

Don Cossacks' reemergence.

Minorities are dubious and

often fearful of this resurgence,

remembering the brutalities

their ancestors suffered during

Cossack pogroms.

NOVOCHERKASSK,

RUSSIA 1992

Captivated by Cossack
splendor, a young girl watches
soldiers parade past. Trained
from childhood to stand on the
sidelines, Cossack women are
relegated to the roles of cook,
mother, housekeeper, and wife.

DIVNOMORSKOYE,

RUSSIA 1997

To learn the traditions and discipline of Cossackhood, boys attend Cossack summer camp. Such camps fill the void left by the Young Pioneer Communist camps. Unlike them, these are blessed by an Orthodox priest.

KRASNODAR,

RUSSIA 2001

Easter midnight Mass at St.

Yekatarina's overflows with

worshipers of all ages and

social backgrounds. The Mass's

culmination comes as priests

lead a procession around

the cathedral.

MOSCOW 1997

*Founded in 1282, Danilov
Monastery claims to be the
city's oldest. Official residence
of the Russian Orthodox patri-
arch, it boasts a surprisingly
modern and businesslike air,
reflecting the Orthodox
Church's prestige and influence
in the New Russia.*

ANTIPOVKA,

RUSSIA 1997

*In a communal spirit, friends
and family help a farmer and
his recently widowed mother
harvest hay in a small farming
community near the Don River
in southern Russia.*

MOSKOVSKOYE,

RUSSIA 1997

A Gypsy woman sells prize pork parts at a market in the Caucasus. This fertile mountain region historically has been home to many ethnic groups, and tensions among them are once again flaring.

129

DON RIVER,

RUSSIA 1997

After a sunset bath, horse and

rider rear from the waters of

the fabled Don.

VLADIVOSTOK,

RUSSIA 1996

Children play at a beach on the Sea of Japan, one of Russia's few stretches of warm-water coast. During the Soviet era families flocked here on company-paid holidays—a luxury lost in the new economy.

STAROCHERKASSK,

RUSSIA 1997

After some lighthearted

folk dancing, picnickers refuel

with a robust meal—and lots

of vodka.

KIEV, UKRAINE 1992

Following Western ways, people in the former Soviet republics have embraced a newfound body consciousness. At Hydropark Beach, even nude sunbathing is given a modest try.

MOSCOW 1992

Entertaining diehards, a lone

woman performs for a crowd of

communists gathered in Gorky

Park to await the appearance

of their leader—Gennady

Zyuganov. He never showed.

NOVOSIBIRSK,
RUSSIA 1996

View on the New Russia:
A car's windshield, held in
place by coins, frames a
woman dressed to kill and a
roadside sign reading, "The new
generation chooses freedom."

MOSCOW 1996

Suspended above the warren of

antiques, souvenirs, and

oriental carpets that make up

the Izmaylovo Market, a car

looms as a symbol of modernity.

MOSCOW 1992

Hundreds of imported TVs,

stereos, and VCRs, move

through the open-air

Bagrationovsky Market on

weekends. As with most

businesses, these vendors pay

protection money to the

"roof"—mafia gangs.

139

MOSCOW 1996

A model struts the latest stuff at a Moscow nightclub. When state-controlled fashion ended, a new generation of Russian designers rushed to the rescue. This gown, part of Elena Soupron's first collection, reflects the changing times in its price tag—a modest $5,000.

ST. PETERSBURG,

RUSSIA 1992

Amped by punk music, thugs

beat each other up at the Tam-

Tam Club. Promoter Seva

Gakkel says, "I'd rather they

come here for a good time than

assault people on the subway."

MOSCOW 1996

Nightclub to day club. Shut down as too noisy by night, the Ptuch reopened for daytime ravers. At a late afternoon fashion show, the audience enjoys the latest vogue— transvestite models.

KIEV, UKRAINE 1992

A young artist poses for a fellow

painter in a studio alive with

punk rock music and

counter-culture ambitions,

both still considered outré by

traditional Russian society.

MOSCOW 1992

Hitler for hire: An actor paid to mingle with the guests at a chic Moscow party is a stunning sight in a country where so many millions suffered during the Nazi invasion of World War II.

MOSCOW 1996

*Reviving the European salon
tradition, poets gather to share
their works. Freely versing,
one writer recites a poem that
cost him his teaching job in
1986. Now he shares his poetry
with millions via newspaper,
radio, and television.*

MOSCOW 1996

On the Frunzenskaya
Embankment, Muscovites
pause along the Moscow River,
in view of Christ the Savior's
glinting new domes.

MOSCOW 1996

Five years after the fall of communism, chic malls like the restored Petrovsky Passaj offer newly affluent Muscovites all kinds of luxury goods produced in the West.

VLADIVOSTOK,

RUSSIA 1996

After a run of thousands of

miles, the Trans-Siberian

Railroad reaches the end of the

line on the Vladivostok water-

front, also home to the Russian

Navy's Pacific Fleet.

151

MOSCOW 1996

A sun worshiper ignores the last vestiges of winter and embraces the return of sunshine. To stay in shape, many Russians swim in the icy waters of winter, a long-cherished method for rejuvenating the body.

THREE THE SHAPE OF THE NEW

Twelve years after I first arrived in Russia, I once again found myself driving from Sheremetyevo Airport to downtown Moscow along the Leningrad Highway. It was a brilliant, cold, January day with deep snow covering the fields north of the capital and an azure sky overhead, a stark contrast to the gloomy scene that greeted me in November 1989. Not far from Sheremetyevo, I passed a monument from the Soviet era—rust-colored tank traps marking the line where the Red Army halted the German advance in the winter of 1941. Just past that memorial, I looked west and saw, 200 hundred yards from the highway, another monument, this one to 21st-century Russia—an enormous blue-and-yellow building that houses the country's first IKEA store.

Anyone who doubts that a middle class is slowly emerging in Russia need only make a weekend pilgrimage to this temple of moderately priced Scandinavian style, as I did on a Sunday afternoon a few days later. I stood in the packed parking lot and watched as a throng of Muscovites—20,000 descended on the store that day—hauled all manner of beds, sofas, bookshelves, cabinets, kitchen sinks, dishes, and other doodads out of IKEA. To my great relief, the shoppers were not, for the most part, the "new Russians" so visible in Moscow in the mid-1990s: Closely shorn men who looked like prizefighters, accompanied by women so dolled up they made prostitutes seem matronly by comparison. Instead, flocking to IKEA that January day were what might be called "new new Russians," people who worked in banks, small businesses, travel agencies, and computer companies; ordinary citizens whose gains were not, for the most part, ill-gotten. In short, these were members of a new middle class that, in the estimate of sociologists, makes up about 20 percent of Moscow's 8.6 million people. They generally live in households with a monthly income of at least a thousand dollars, and chances are good that they have seen hip advertisements for IKEA on television—ads that depict young couples in decrepit, Soviet-style apartments, then show them spicing up their lives, IKEA style.

Amid the towering shelves of IKEA's self-serve warehouse, a young couple—Andrei Dmitrienkov and Tatiana Dyakonova—were stacking their metal shopping cart high with hutches and baby furniture, all in preparation for a child due any day. Andrei is a product manager for a company that sells computer parts and Tatiana is a teacher who, in her spare time, operates two stores that sell food and cosmetics. Together, they make a few thousand dollars a month, which puts them at the upper end of Moscow's middle class. Yet, given the economic crises they had endured in Russia's first decade of capitalism—ruble devaluations, runaway inflation—they displayed an understandable caution.

"I feel some optimism, but things are still a mess," said Andrei. "We've been going through a terrible, extortionate phase of capitalism. Maybe life will be more normal for our grandchildren."

For those of us who remember the bad old days—two-block-long lines for imported Czech shoes and salespeople who were the personification of boorishness—Moscow's IKEA verges on the hallucinatory. As I stood there, watching fashionably dressed young couples caress $350 couches and saleswomen answer inquiries with a smile, I asked myself: Am I really in Russia? But the real proof that something had changed was in the store's bathroom, a gleaming expanse of white tiles and clean sinks. Only Soviet veterans could appreciate this pristine pissoir, for almost without exception public bathrooms in the U.S.S.R. had been unspeakable. About the only clean restroom I encountered in three-and-a-half years was the one at the Congress of People's Deputies, the Soviet parliament, where the high-living Communist Party bosses relieved themselves in sparkling white urinals created by Villeroy and Boche. I don't want to make too much of IKEA's lovely bathroom, but it seemed to me a sign of progress that Russians had managed to keep a public space in such fine working order.

In the spring and summer of 2001, I crisscrossed Russia in search of more new life, more signs that the country was building something resembling a civil society and a market economy. It seemed a tidy time to make such a trip, a decade after the historic year that witnessed the failed coup in August and the official demise of the U.S.S.R. on December 25, 1991. I discovered that the situation in Russia was wildly mixed—not nearly as gloomy as most armchair pontificators in Moscow and Washington made it sound, yet still a very long way from a humane market system. I also learned that what you found depended on where you looked. If you were searching for shoots of new life, they were abundant, and not just in Moscow. In other large cities—St. Petersburg, Samara, Nizhniy Novgorod, Yekaterinburg, Novosibirsk, Irkutsk—businesses were springing up in sectors that scarcely had existed in the Soviet Union, like high-tech and food packaging. In the Siberian town of Akademgorodok, home to three dozen of the former U.S.S.R.'s finest research institutions, dozens of computer businesses employing thousands of people had been created in the past few years. In the industrial, Ural Mountain city of Chelyabinsk, entrepreneurs had opened a modern, two-theater movie, arcade, and restaurant complex that had pulled in 600,000 visitors in its first year. In southern Russia, successful farmers were establishing such businesses as flour mills, and food-processing companies were investing in anemic collective farms to boost production. A small middle class, probably no more than 10 percent of the population, was emerging in the provinces and slowly growing.

But if you were searching for signs of gloom, you didn't have to go far. Most Russian workers still earn pitifully low wages, about $100 per month. More than 30 million of Russia's 145 million people live below the official poverty line of $30 a person per month. Tax evasion is still epidemic, and an estimated 25 to 40 percent of the economy is conducted underground. And every year, a tiny layer of super-rich Russians exports an estimated $20 to $25 billion worth of goods, much of it from the sale of Russia's abundant natural resources.

On the social side, the statistics don't look much better. Life expectancy has fallen sharply since the Soviet era, peaking for men in 1985 at 65 years old, dropping in 1994 to a low of 58, then climbing back to 61 in 2001. At the start of the 21st century, the life span of the average Russian man was 12 years shorter than that of either an American man or a Russian women. Such high male death rates are due in large part to smoking and rampant alcoholism. Couple them with a drop in the birth rate as Russian women have fewer children in tough times and you have a country with one of the fastest shrinking populations on Earth. Russia's current population of 145 million is expected to fall to 137 million in 2025 and 128 million by the middle of the 21st century.

But behind the grim facts and figures, Russia in 2001 presented a picture that was anything but black and white. My travels convinced me of a few things. First, that what was percolating from the bottom up in Russian society was far more heartening than what was coming from the top down. Second, that while Russia's institutions—courts, federal and local legislatures, banks—were often a mess, many individual Russians were gradually building a more civilized society. And last, far more so than in most other countries, young people were driving the positive changes taking place in Russia. Hang around with a group of 50-year-old factory workers and you're soon prepared to read Russia her last rites. But spend a few days with well-educated young Russians and you start to feel pretty good about the place.

AT THE TOP of the Russian heap these days is Vladimir V. Putin, a 48-year-old former KGB colonel who, to his misfortune, looks the part. Short, wiry, with a long, doleful face, ski-slope nose and shifty eyes, Russia's new president is the antithesis of his lumbering, stormy predecessor, Boris Yeltsin. Reformers love to hate Putin, fearing he will quash democracy and bring back the days when the security services had a free hand. Putin revived the war in Chechnya; resurrected the Soviet anthem; co-opted almost all the political opposition; and, most liberals believe, orchestrated the takeover of the independent station, NTV, by the state-controlled oil and gas corporation, Gazprom.

"We have an elected monarchy, where Putin was elected president but where he has created a political desert with no rivals," Lilia Shevtsova, a senior associate at the Carnegie Moscow Center, told me.

I visited a number of the reformers I had known a decade before, and none was more amusing, or philosophical, than Boris Nemtsov, one of the wunderkinder of perestroika. I had first met Nemtsov in 1991, not long after he had been elected governor of Nizhniy Novgorod at age 30. He was an apostle of shock therapy and, after being made one of Yeltsin's deputy prime ministers, tried—with utter lack of success—to force the country to reform the electric utility system, which was heavily subsidized by the government and slowly disintegrating. Yeltsin eventually sacked Nemtsov, as the president did with nearly all his ministers. But the young reformer rebounded, and, when I visited him in January 2001, he was the leader of the liberal opposition in the Russian Duma.

I hadn't seen Nemtsov in six or seven years, but he had changed little. He was still a tall, handsome man with curly dark hair, a mischievous grin, and a wide streak of irreverence. I tried to walk him down memory lane, to the heady days of the Soviet democratic movement, but he preferred not to linger too long on the past.

"It was a romantic time," he told me as we sat in his spacious, wood-paneled office in the duma on a frigid Saturday afternoon. "We all expected miracles."

Soon, our conversation turned to Putin. "You want to know the difference between Putin and Yeltsin?" said Nemtsov, scooping up peanuts from a bowl and throwing them into his mouth. "Yeltsin had two main principles. That freedom is better than communism. And that private ownership is better than bureaucracy and government ownership. Putin, it seems to me, has no such principles. In his career Yeltsin didn't touch the press. He often hated the press, because a lot of reporters criticized him. But what was his idea of fighting the press? To switch off the TV."

Nemtsov views Putin the way many other reformers did—as a timid bureaucrat afraid to tackle tough issues like corruption and judicial reform, all because he fears tarnishing his 70 percent approval rating.

"Russia's like a rusty ship," said Nemtsov. "It's barely floating, and, instead of trying to repair the ship in fundamental ways, Putin just grabs a bucket of paint and starts painting it in patriotic colors. That's the essence of Putin. He won't do anything fundamental. The security services, the police, the prosecutors, he won't touch these elements of the Soviet system."

Nemtsov acknowledged that Putin—who had almost no political experience before Yeltsin appointed him prime minister, then annointed him as his successor—might grow into the job. And it would be foolish to write Putin off as a weaselly, ex-spook intent on bringing back the repression of the Soviet Union. Like Yeltsin, Putin supports a market economy, but unlike Yeltsin, Putin is young, sober, and energetic. I talked to businessmen who had met him, and they came away impressed with his desire to create conditions for a more normal market economy. Even the event that most alarmed liberals, Gazprom's takeover of NTV, is not as simple as it looks at first glance. Most reformers and Western observers painted the NTV affair as Putin's attempt to silence the station, which had been his most powerful critic. No doubt there was some truth to this scenario. Yet what received little notice in the Western press was that even NTV journalists were split, with a minority viewing the fight more as a corporate takeover battle. NTV's primary owner, Vladimir Gusinsky, was deeply in debt to Gazprom, and the oil and gas giant was merely laying claim to its rightful asset, according to the dissenting NTV journalists.

"Free speech at our stage of development as a state is always a test," Tatiana Mitkova, one of NTV's premier anchors, told me just days before Gazprom took control of the station. "The problem is that we haven't yet learned to combine free speech and a market economy. Now we're experiencing a change of ownership in accordance with the laws of the market. No one is taking away freedom of speech."

ATTEMPTING TO FIND CLARITY in the murk of Kremlin intrigues is a frustrating experience that never held much interest for me. I always found that jettisoning Russian politics and poking around in the real world—factories, farms, businesses—was a far more enlightening and edifying exercise. I did that in the beginning months of 2001, looking particularly for successful enterprises run by young Russians. I found them in profusion, and, after spending a couple of weeks in the presence of these 20- and 30-something entrepreneurs, I had to remind myself how profoundly Russia had changed in just a decade, and how easy it is to ignore the progress if you focus on the daunting problems facing the country. Of course, the time comes when you have to step off these islands of youthful success and into the rest of Russia, a land of colossal corruption, prolific drunkenness, and institutions perverted by seven decades of communism and centuries of backwardness. But this is the challenge of understanding the country today: to hold in your head the dichotomy of the two Russias. One is a place of well-educated, savvy people, many of them young, building a decent society; the other a land where a passive, worn-out populace watches angrily as crooks plunder a vast trove of natural resources. The dissident Soviet writer Fasil Iskander put it nicely when he said that everything in Russia has changed, and everything has remained the same. The question today is, will the second Russia inevitably overwhelm the first, or will the New Russia slowly spread and, in the course of several generations, ultimately prevail?

Russia has fooled me before—I was far too optimistic in the early 1990s—and I am reluctant now to make a guess. But Anatoliy Karachinskiy, the country's most successful computer entrepreneur, is betting on the New Russia. His company, the IBS Group, is typical of those businesses that didn't even exist in the Soviet Union but have enjoyed tremendous growth in recent years, as the Russian economy has stopped its free fall and begun to expand. (Gross domestic product increased almost 8 percent in 2000 and is expected to rise by 4 percent in 2001.) Karachinsky is the anti-oligarch. A computer nut during the Soviet days, he saw a niche in the new economy and occupied it. As capitalism took its first, lurching steps, Karachinsky began to design and install the sophisticated computer systems that integrate the operations of large businesses. The deal that launched his IBS group was the overhaul of computer operations at Sberbank, the national savings bank that has 25,000 branches. By 2000 he was working with Russian giants like Gazprom and foreign firms like Ford. IBS's revenues have been increasing by 50 percent a year, and Karachinsky now employs nearly 2,000 people, almost all of them under 40.

I spent a half day with Karachinsky in IBS's glass-and-concrete office building on the industrial Dmitrovskoye Highway in Moscow. He's an unpretentious man of 41, with reddish-brown hair and a well-trimmed beard to match. On the day I met him, he was wearing khakis and cowboy boots, hardly standard attire for one of Russia's business leaders. As Karachinsky explained it, much of the old Soviet industrial sector may indeed fail, but those losses will be offset by an expanding service sector and a burgeoning resource economy, now rapidly modernizing.

"Something entirely new is being born here," he told me. "It's very clear to me that Russia is just at the beginning of an economic climb. For us that's good, because the more the economy develops, the more work and clients for us. I don't see anything getting in the way of Russia's growth. It's the richest country in the world and I think that for the next 10 to 12 years we'll have political stability.... Overall, I'm pretty optimistic."

Karachinsky has hired some of the best talent in Russia, several of them graduates of such U.S. business schools as Harvard's and the University of Pennsylvania's Wharton School. One of his top managers, Dmitry Loschinin, heads up the rapidly growing subsidiary, Luxoft, which does computer programming for foreign firms like Boeing. In just two years, Luxoft has grown from 150 to nearly 400 employees, many of them in their late 20s. Most are housed in an adjacent, renovated factory, where they sit in long rows, earning the princely sum of up to a thousand dollars a month as they provide computer solutions for the world.

"Even though many people are still suffering economically, there is tremendous improvement between where we are now in Russia and where we were five years ago," said Loschinin, a handsome 34-year-old in a well-tailored, three-button gray suit. "Yes, this operation is like an island, but this island is growing, and pretty soon all these islands will turn into a mainland."

I visited other such islands throughout Russia. Akademgorodok, 1,800 miles east of Moscow, is home to Siberia's greatest collection of research institutions. In the early to mid-1990s, as state funding evaporated, many scientists fled Akademgorodok for the West in a massive brain drain. But that hemorrhaging is now being staunched as mathematicians, physicists, and computer specialists form so many high-tech companies that the city is known as "silicon taiga."

Russia's new economy involves a lot more than computers, though. Indeed, one of the most robust sectors is food processing and packaging, given a major boost after the financial crisis of 1998, when the ruble collapsed. It lost four times its value in relation to the dollar, a loss that hammered the fledgling middle class. But the crisis soon began to have a positive effect: Imports became prohibitively expensive, and Russian-based producers of food and consumer goods stepped in to fill the gap.

In my dozen years in Russia, I have watched the country's infatuation with Western goods change dramatically. When the economy first opened up in the early 1990s, Russians were mad for things Western—McDonald's, Snickers, Dannon yogurt, imported French cheeses, and German hams. But by 2001, not only could many Russians not afford most foreign foods, they also had grown tired of this outside invasion and were taking pride in their domestic products, whose quality had improved exponentially. I, too, had become a convert. Russian sausages and processed meats were far more delicious than the tasteless slices of indefinable plastic material that passed for ham or turkey in the U.S.

To many Russian workers, though, these culinary improvements make little difference. For them, the changes of the past decade have brought pain and a drop in living standards. In the Soviet era, nearly everyone belonged to a shabby middle class. The food wasn't great, the clothes were worse, and cars and apartments took years to procure. But workers earned enough to enjoy a summer vacation on the Black Sea, the future seemed more or less stable, and—this was the great consolation—almost everyone was in the same boat. All that has changed in a decade, and today many workers struggle to survive on a hundred dollars a month. For these people, vacations are a distant memory, and most rely on extensive summer gardens to keep them supplied with potatoes and pickled vegetables through the winter. What galls them most, however, is the knowledge that a small number of well-connected businessmen and criminals have become obscenely rich, while workers like themselves have slid toward poverty.

For many, particularly the middle-aged and elderly, Russia's ten-year leap into the capitalist world has been a profoundly disillusioning experience. The promise of Mikhail Gorbachev and *perestroika*—freedom of expression, the arrival, at long last, of prosperity, and an end to the reign of corrupt Communist Party bosses—now seems little more than a bitter joke.

At the Chelyabinsk Tractor Factory, an industrial giant in the Soviet era that cranked out its first tractor in 1933 and produced tanks for the Soviet Army in World War II, workers and managers are reeling from a ten-fold drop in production. Men on the assembly line are relieved to be making a hundred dollars a month, having experienced a period in the mid-1990s when one set of owners nearly drove the factory into bankruptcy and didn't pay salaries for a half year. The frustrations of the Chelyabinsk collective were voiced by Khanif Mingasov, 58, deputy director of the plant.

"All our lives we worked hard to strengthen our army and the economy, and now to produce so little with all our skills, it's insulting," Mingasov told me. "Economic reforms were needed, but they were not well thought out. On the one hand our leaders said revolution was no good, but on the other hand we allowed super-revolutionary changes. For our generation these changes have been a big spiritual trauma. To say we are creating a democracy but at the same time drive the economy so low—well, it's good to be able to speak freely, but you also have to eat."

MINGAZOV AND HIS WORKERS stand at the opposite extreme of computer entrepreneur Karachinsky and his team of young, high-tech employees. One business is a relic from the Soviet past, struggling to stay afloat in a capitalist economy, while the other is a symbol of Russia's ability to flourish in a new world. When you look closely at the men and women in both companies, what most shapes their outlook is a sense of control, or lack of it. Karachinsky and the people at IBS feel that they are in charge of their destiny, whereas the men on the assembly line at the Chelyabinsk Tractor Factory sense they are adrift in a system indifferent to their fate.

The momentum in Russia these days is with the likes of Karachinsky. But after a dozen years of observing Russia, I've learned that it's wise not to get too fired up about one prospect or another. When speaking of Russia, it's best to leave ideas of optimism and pessimism out of the discussion. The country is what it is: An enormous land, with little tradition of democracy or capitalism, undergoing enormous changes in a short period of time. It is a confounding place, a territory of almost limitless resources and low living standards, a nation of resilient, admirable people who perpetually seem to be trapped in a system unworthy of their kind.

Today, I feel the same wonder I experienced 12 years ago when I drove down Moscow's wide, dismal boulevards for the first time and saw the red stars floating above the Kremlin. Russia continues to exert a pull over me for many reasons, but one of them undoubtedly is this: After all these years, I'm still not sure which way it's going to go. ■

MOSCOW 2000

Christmas makes a comeback:
Repressed under the atheistic
communists, holiday festivities
now blanket Moscow with sea-
sonal cheer. At the gates to Red
Square, vendors costumed as
Father Frost, the Russian ver-
sion of Santa, hawk Cokes
to New Year's Eve revelers.

CHI, RUSSIA 2001

Russians—probably part

ne affluent mafia crowd—

or an old tradition:

hering to wine and dine at

grave of a deceased relative

Parent's Day, the second

sday after Easter.

YAKUTSK, RUSSIA 2001

Accustomed to violent winters, women in the Sakha Republic keep warm in floor-length furs. Thanks to its rich natural resources, Russia's remote northern province harbors islands of prosperity—but not warmth. In January, the daily high in the capital, Yakutsk, averages minus 43°F.

ST. PETERSBURG,

RUSSIA 2001

At the Russian Academy of
Science, Vladimir Putin stands
surrounded by scientists and
bodyguards. A puzzle to
political pundits, Putin was
raised Orthodox, but rose
through the ranks of the KGB.
Joining with reformers, he was
handpicked by Yeltsin and
elected to Russia's highest office
in 1999.

MOSCOW 1996

Newly renovated, the century-

old Belinsky Building in the

city center boasts rents among

the highest in the world.

Western companies hungry for

downtown Moscow space

financed the renovations.

ST. PETERSBURG,

RUSSIA 2001

The shadowy shape of Feliks

Dzerzhinsky, infamous founder

of the KGB, still hovers close

by Smolny Cathedral, used as

headquarters by the Bolsheviks

in the 1918 revolution. Most

Dzerzhinsky statues have been

toppled since the fall of commu-

nism, but this one survives.

MOSCOW 2001

Military might and majesty are rehearsed in preparation for the May 9—Victory Day—parade commemorating the end of World War II. Today, for the first time in its history, Russia has appointed a civilian minister of defense—another sign of changing times.

**NIZHNIY NOVGOROD,
RUSSIA 2001**

*During lunch break at GAZ
(the Gorkovsky auto plant),
welders relax over a board
game. Built in 1929, the plant,
one of Russia's largest car
producers, is now largely
outdated. Plans to update its
equipment were stymied by the
economic crisis in 1998.*

NORILSK,

RUSSIA 2001

At Norilsk Nickel business booms, and the hard times of the early 1990s seem distant memories. Then, this city, one of the largest above the Arctic Circle, lost population as factories stagnated. Now copper and nickel production have risen dramatically, and so have wages.

NORILSK,

RUSSIA 2001

A river of liquid slag lights the

Arctic night, the spectacular

sight belying the damage done

by the refuse from nickel and

copper smelters.

NISHNEVARTOVSK,

RUSSIA 2001

In the permafrosted swamps of western Siberia, the Samotlor oil field, one of the world's richest, guards its wealth with subzero, subhuman conditions.

EDEITSY,

RUSSIA 2001

Yakut villagers dip water for

cattle from their "well," a

frozen lake that serves as the

only source of water. Like most

Russian villages in the

permafrosted far north, this

one lacks running water.

NOVOSIBIRSK,

RUSSIA 2001

Rooftop romp: Undaunted by

their frigid world, two boys

leap from a roof into mounds

of deep, soft snow.

183

YAKUTSK,

RUSSIA 2001

New dachas on the outskirts
of Yakutsk, capital of the
Sakha Republic, herald the
area's recent prosperity.
Blanketing a fifth of Russia
and rich in diamonds, the
republic has wrested a limited
autonomy from the central
government, but relations
between the two are strained.

YAKUTSK,

RUSSIA 2001

Out for a ride, children take
a turn around Yakutsk's Lenin
Square, still overseen by a stat-
ue of the revolutionary father.

YAKUTSK,

RUSSIA 2001

Flash frozen by the ambient

temperature, fish and meat

await buyers browsing quickly

through an outdoor market.

MOSCOW 2001

Russia's new elite dine in first-

class splendor at the Café

Pushkin, where a bottle of wine

can cost as much as $2,800.

MOSCOW 2001

*Toasting the New Year, family
and friends gather for an all-
night party. Since Russians
toggle between two calendars—
the Julian for secular life and
the Gregorian for Orthodox
holidays—most employers
honor both by closing from
December 24 to mid-January.*

YAKUTSK,

RUSSIA 2001

With his work day over, a

father helps his son with

English homework. Even in this

remote Siberian town, English

comes in handy in his line of

work—driving a cab.

ST. PETERSBURG,

RUSSIA 2001

One of the city's thousands of bomzhi—homeless—this elderly woman may be among those who lost their apartments due to property swindles. Without a home, a Russian loses the right to work, to a pension, to medical care, even to a passport.

NORILSK,
RUSSIA 2001

A classic Slavic beauty,

lost in thought

NOVOSIBIRSK,
RUSSIA 2001

New York Pizza Restaurant,
a fast-food first in this city,
has been a teen hotspot since
it was established in the mid-
1990s. Its American owner has
now expanded his operations to
include several new businesses
in Novosibirsk.

ST. PETERSBURG,

RUSSIA 2001

Bearing the marks of abuse, a
homeless mother comes with
her children for the twice-
weekly hot meal offered at a
Moscow shelter. Ten years ago,
homelessness was classified by
the government as a crime,
rather than a human tragedy.

MOSCOW 2001

Disinfection Center #2 in Lianozovo, a Moscow suburb, treats increasing numbers of underprivileged sufferers of infectious diseases. Many come voluntarily, but militia also rounds up the homeless and delivers them to such centers.

MOSCOW 2001

*Only 28, designer Masha Tsigal
has already made a name for
herself in the burgeoning
Russian fashion world. Trained
in fashion marketing in
England, Masha has claimed
red high heels as a trademark
of her "Bloody Mary" look.*

NOVOSIBIRSK,

RUSSIA 2001

Well-wrapped Siberian

shoppers make their way from

the Baraholka Market,

oblivious to a billboard whose

advertising seems better aimed

at a different clime.

ST. PETERSBURG,
RUSSIA 2001

Arguably the most famous street in Russia, Nevsky Prospect was cut through forest land in the early 1700s. Now, in the early 2000s, it has become a forest of billboards—though plans are under way to limit their numbers.

NOVOSIBIRSK,
RUSSIA 2001

The Internet Club, a teen

hangout, has become this city's

most popular cyber café.

Overall in Russia, there is only

one computer per hundred peo-

ple, but sales of PCs are rising.

MOSCOW 2001

MTV Russian began airing in 1999, broadcasting on the culture channel by night. A hit from the start, it draws more teenage viewers than any other offering on television.

MOSCOW 2000

Cell phone in hand, a young beauty contemplates the strollers that now crowd Manezhnaya Square. Until a recent restoration, there was very little foot traffic.

ST. PETERSBURG,

RUSSIA 2001

On Dvortsovaya Square, in
front of the tsars' former Winter
Palace, young people collect for
a late afternoon ritual of in-line
skating, gossiping, and just
hanging out.

MOSCOW 1992

Male dancers entertain an

appreciative female audience at

the Little Red Riding Hood,

one of Moscow's new breed of

all-night clubs.

NOVOSIBIRSK,

RUSSIA 2001

Doing business, Russian style,

means doing banya—*even for*

an American entrepreneur.

This ritualized marathon of

sauna-sitting, bathing, eating,

drinking, playing games—

and drinking some more—

establishes personal "credit"

and oils the wheels of business.

MOSCOW,

RUSSIA 2001

At an erotic nightclub, semi-

nude young men entertain

customers by swimming in a

lighted tank, as classical music

accompanies their movements.

NOVOSIBIRSK,

RUSSIA 2001

Siberian hipness: At the New

York Times, a club founded

by an American entrepreneur,

locals and foreigners mix to

the beat of blues, jazz, and

rock music.

ST. PETERSBURG,

RUSSIA 1992

*Where communist heroes
once hovered, capitalist advertising now proclaims itself.
On this billboard a candy
called* Rossya—Russia—
*tempts the passing world with
its "generous soul."*

ACKNOWLEDGMENTS

A few years ago, over dinner and a good bottle of wine, Lisa Lytton, David Griffin, and I first came up with the idea for this book—a ten-year retrospective of my work in the former Soviet Union. Lisa went on to become my editor and David created the elegant design. I could not have asked for more talented collaborators.

Many of the people I first met at the Geographic in the course of this work shared their time and effort with me and became close friends. I am grateful to the magazine's editor, Bill Allen, director of photography Kent Kobersteen, and assistant director of photography Susan Smith for allowing me to pursue my interests in the former Soviet Union by assigning me to that part of the world. And to former NATIONAL GEOGRAPHIC editor Bill Graves and former director of photography Tom Kennedy, who initially sent me to the U.S.S.R. in 1991 to document the changes.

As a photographer in the field, I very much depend on the collaboration and feedback from my picture editors at National Geographic headquarters. I can hardly find the words to thank Susan Welchman for her commitment to my work. She was there for endless long-distance calls, providing guidance on film sent from the field, bombarding me with ideas, and steering me out of dead ends. Thank you Susan for your vision. My thanks also to Dennis Dimick, who helped me edit stories at a difficult time in my career. And thanks to director of illustrations W. Allan Royce, who graciously gave me access to all of my photographs for use in this book.

Every book is a leap of faith, and I would like to thank the Book Division's president, Nina Hoffman, vice president and editor-in-chief Kevin Mulroy, and illustrations editor Charles Kogod for giving the project team the freedom to pursue our vision.

I am grateful to my illustrations editor, Sadie Quarrier, for coming to Los Angeles and helping me sift through hundreds of images as we began the process of shaping the book. And thanks to K. M. Kostyal, my text editor, for structuring, streamlining, and polishing what could have been a linguistic nightmare, were it not for my eloquent and resourceful assistant, Liz Cavalier.

My appreciation to Fen Montaigne for his enthusiasm for the project and his informative, energetic text, and to Tatyana Tolstaya for her insightful foreword.

Many photographers around the world are an inspiration to me, especially my National Geographic friends and colleagues, David Alan Harvey and Bill Allard who have raised the bar with their recent retrospective works for the National Geographic.

I would like to thank the many people who worked on the production of this book, especially John Dunn, Carl Mehler, and Tony Shugaar.

Thanks to National Geographic Society president and CEO John Fahey, executive vice president Terry Adamson, and senior associate editor Connie Phelps; to Leah Bendavid-Val, Luda Mekertycheva, Elena Bespalova, Kathy Moran, Tom O'Neill, Mike Davis, Memo Zack, Frank Evers, Joel Newman, David Schonauer, Jean-Jacques Naudet; to NATIONAL GEOGRAPHIC's research and legends departments, especially to Hillel Hoffmann; and to the staff and photographers of Visum, my agency in Germany.

I am thankful for always being able to turn to George Steinmetz for his practical advice on logistics and technical wizardry. His innovative and physical approach to photography leaves me in awe.

Thank you to my friend and confidante Lauren Greenfield—her depth and intellectual reflection on photography as well as her stimulating grasp of the conceptual elements of photography have become a constant source of inspiration.

I am grateful to my dear, longtime friends Douglas and Françoise Kirkland, for supporting me at every step of my career while generously opening their home. A legendary photographer, Douglas constantly impresses me with his enthusiasm, energy, versatility, and curiosity. Always searching for perfection, Douglas encouraged me to use Canon cameras in my photography, which in turn led to my introduction to Michael Newler to whom I am grateful for selecting me as one of Canon's Explorers of Light.

Without the tireless efforts of Maxim Kusnetsov, who has been my assistant and interpreter since my first assignment in Russia, this book would have been impossible. I am completely indebted to Maxim for his loyalty and unflagging endurance, for pushing me to see his country through the Russian soul, eye, and experience, and for introducing me to his network of friends, especially to Sergey Resanov, who worked on several assignments as my resourceful stringer.

I want to thank my father, whose life story inspired my work, and my mother, whose unconditional love, support, encouragement, and belief in my work was always a source of strength and motivation.

Words are not enough to express my gratitude to my son, Max. Spending time with him let me once again see the world through a child's eye. Thank you Max, your love has become my greatest inspiration.

And my sincerest thanks to the Russian people, who, so often suffering through hardships, welcomed me into their lives with open hearts and showed me their souls.

To them, my parents, and my son, I dedicate this book.

BROKEN EMPIRE: AFTER THE FALL OF THE USSR

PUBLISHED BY
THE NATIONAL GEOGRAPHIC SOCIETY
John M. Fahey, Jr., *President and Chief Executive Officer*
Gilbert M. Grosvenor, *Chairman of the Board*
Nina D. Hoffman, *Executive Vice President*

PREPARED BY THE BOOK DIVISION
Kevin Mulroy, *Vice President and Editor-in-Chief*
Charles Kogod, *Illustrations Director*
Barbara A. Payne, *Editorial Director*
Marianne R. Koszorus, *Design Director*

STAFF FOR THIS BOOK
Lisa Lytton, *Project Editor*
K. M. Kostyal, *Text Editor*
Sadie Quarrier, *Illustrations Editor*
David Griffin, *Art Director*
Carl Mehler, *Director of Maps*
Timothy D. Sergay, *Translator*
Richard Wain, *Production Manager*

Copyright © 2001 National Geographic Society
Photographs © 2001 Gerd Ludwig

All rights reserved. Reproduction of the whole or any part of the contents without permission is prohibited.

Printed in Italy

Library of Congress Cataloging-in-Publication Data

Ludwig, Gerd.
    Broken empire : after the fall of the USSR / photographs by Gerd Ludwig ; text by Fen Montaigne.
        p. cm.
    ISBN 0-7922-6432-0
        1. Russia (Federation)--Social conditions--1991---Pictorial works. 2.
    Post-communism--Russia (Federation)--Pictorial works. I. Ludwig, Gerd, 1947- II.
    Title.
    HN530.2.A8 M66 2001
    306'.0947'0222--dc21
                                                    2001037074

The world's largest nonprofit scientific and educational organization, the National Geographic Society was founded in 1888 "for the increase and diffusion of geographic knowledge." Fulfilling this mission, the Society educates and inspires millions every day through magazines, books, television programs, videos, maps and atlases, research grants, the National Geographic Bee, teacher workshops, and innovative classroom materials. The Society is supported through membership dues, charitable gifts, and income from the sale of its educational products.

Call 1-800-NGS-LINE (647-5463) for more information.

Visit the Society's Web site at www.nationalgeographic.com.